Due	Return	Due	Return
Date	Date	Date	Date

POMPONNE DE BELLIÈVRE

Northwestern University Studies in History
NUMBER FOUR

POMPONNE
DE
BELLIÈVRE

A Study of the King's Men
in the Age of Henry IV

RAYMOND F. KIERSTEAD

Northwestern University Press

1968

The publication of this book has been aided by
contributions from friends of James Alton James.

Raymond F. Kierstead is Assistant Professor
of History at Yale University.

PREFACE

THE FOLLOWING MONOGRAPH was originally prepared as a doctoral dissertation presented to the Department of History of Northwestern University. A University Fellowship, offered by Northwestern University, allowed me to carry out my research in France. I should like to thank Professors Richard M. Brace, George T. Romani, and Alfred Rieber, who read and criticized my work in its initial form. My wife, Marilyn J. Kierstead, worked long hours at the Bibliothèque Nationale during eight hectic months and has since contributed to this study in many ways. The Department of History of Yale University provided funds for the typing of the manuscript, for which I express my gratitude.

My greatest debt is to one of the fine gentlemen of our profession, Professor Gray C. Boyce of Northwestern University. His encouragement and advice have been gratefully received by the author.

R. F. K.

CONTENTS

NOTE   ix

INTRODUCTION   xi

CHAPTER ONE   3
The King's Men: A Collective Portrait

CHAPTER TWO   29
In the Service of Catherine de Medici

CHAPTER THREE   56
The Years at Grignon: 1588–1593

CHAPTER FOUR   75
In the Service of Henry IV: 1594–1599

CHAPTER FIVE   104
His Majesty's Chancellor: 1599–1607

CHAPTER SIX   137
A Robe Dynasty

BIBLIOGRAPHY   149

INDEX   155

$\mathcal{N}OTE$

THE READER'S ATTENTION is called to the following abbreviations of archival sources:

A.N.   ARCHIVES NATIONALES

B.N.   BIBLIOTHÈQUE NATIONALE

Ms. fr.	*Manuscrits français*
Ms. fr., nouv. acq.	*Manuscrits français, nouvelles acquisitions*
PO.	*Pièces originales du Cabinet des Titres*
Cab. H.	*Cabinet de D'Hozier*
Coll. Clair.	*Collection Clairambault*

INTRODUCTION

THE POLITICAL PROBLEM confronting the French monarchy in the second half of the sixteenth century was the basic one of survival. Civil war and religious discord, blatant treason and crippling factionalism threatened to reduce the government of France to a shambles. By the summer of the year 1589, however, it appeared that at last, after a quarter of a century of devastating internal strife, the forces of order and legitimacy represented by King Henry III and his Protestant cousin, Henry of Navarre, were on the verge of a great victory over the Catholic League. But on August 1 of that year a Jacobin friar, Jacques Clément, struck down the King, and the assassin's knife assured that the ultimate victory over the revolutionary league would be the work not of the last surviving son of Henry II, the feckless and neurotic Henry III, but rather of a more able statesman, the King of Navarre. With the murder of the King, at least part of the miserable legacy of Henry II had been liquidated, and a turning point in the history of the country had been reached. When Henry of Navarre claimed the throne, the way was opened for reconciliation and the restoration of order. The new king became the focal point of that spirit of moderation and compromise which during the long years of anarchy had been embodied in the *politiques.*

In the following study, our concern is with the career of a *politique,* administrator, and statesman whose public life spanned the years of the religious wars and culminated in the service of Henry IV. Pomponne de Bellièvre was a pre-eminent figure among those king's men who shared in the governing of France during its time of troubles and who continued to serve the crown in the happier age of the first Bourbon monarch. A spiritual heir of the sixteenth century's greatest political moderate, Michel de L'Hôpital, Bellièvre displayed in his public service and in his writings a passion for order and legitimacy. In an age of turmoil, characterized by disloyalty to crown and country, Bellièvre was a loyalist and rightly thought of himself as a patriot. When he entered the government of Henry IV in 1593, there lay behind him more than thirty years of experience as magistrate, councillor of state, diplomat, and administrator. As councillor and then as chancellor, Bellièvre joined with a select group of crown servants to form an administrative elite which, under the king's direction, carried the major burden of overseeing the kingdom's affairs.

This account of Bellièvre's career is not designed simply to revive the reputation of a statesman who, in an age excessively fond of classical allusions, was hailed as the Nestor of his century.[1] Although an unpublished thesis and a valuable article have illuminated certain aspects of his life,[2] Bellièvre has typically appeared in the literature on the wars of religion as an important, but somewhat obscure, individual flitting about France and traveling abroad in the service of the crown. And it is as a study of a crown servant that this monograph is conceived. Given the present state of research in French administrative history, a field long constricted by an abstractly institutional approach, there is a pressing need for studies which explore the relationship between institutions and the personnel who manned the chief positions in the king's service and which treat the personal, political, and social dimensions of public administration under the Old Regime. In the classic works of Commines, the Duke of Saint-Simon, and Tocqueville, we encounter those men of humble or bourgeois origins who were the agents of absolutism and the creatures of despots. This caricature of the king's men, applied indiscriminately to Capetian, Valois, and Bourbon governments alike, has rightly been rejected by historians. The publications of Orest Ranum, N. M. Sutherland, and François Bluche, among others, have deepened our

1. Breghot du Lut, *Catalogue des lyonnais dignes de mémoire* (Lyons, 1839), p. 31.

2. Louis Monnier, "Les Missions diplomatiques de Pomponne de Bellièvre de 1573 à 1588," *Ecole Nationale des Chartes, positions des thèses* (Paris, 1930), pp. 119–28; Roland Mousnier, "Sully et Le Conseil d'état et des finances: la lutte entre Bellièvre et Sully," *Revue historique*, CXLII (1941), pp. 68–86.

understanding of the administrative service in the early modern era and have given some substance to those faceless creatures who carried out the kingdom's business.[3] We are still far, however, from a thorough knowledge of the great administrators of the *ancien régime*.

Bellièvre was such a figure, and the Chancellor's papers constitute a fundamental source on the administrative sector of the royal court during the late sixteenth and early seventeenth centuries. Although the focus of the following chapters is upon the political and administrative roles of a single high officer of state, an attempt has been made to evoke the total environment within which Bellièvre performed his good services for the crown. The story of the Chancellor's life and public career cannot be separated either from the history of those administrative and magisterial dynasties which dominated royal institutions in the absolutist period or from the history of the monarchy itself. What follows, then, is court history rather than biography. The first chapter seeks to place Bellièvre and his family in the dynamic and close-knit society of officeholders; the remaining chapters examine, in rough chronological sequence, his relations with the crown, the overmighty subjects of the realm, and the *robe longue*.

3. Orest Ranum, *Richelieu and the Councillors of Louis XIII* (Oxford, 1963); N. M. Sutherland, *The French Secretaries of State in the Age of Catherine de Medici* (London, 1962); François Bluche, "L'Origine sociale des secrétaires d'état de Louis XIV, 1661–1715," XVII° siècle, Nos. 42–43 (1959), pp. 8–22.

POMPONNE DE BELLIÈVRE

CHAPTER ONE

The King's Men:
A Collective Portrait

THE DECADES between the death of King Henry II and Cardinal Richelieu's rise to power formed a period of discontinuity in French history which was reflected politically in the general instability of the central government. The chaos of the religious wars, the tragic and occasionally bizarre characters of the last Valois kings, the violent death of Henry IV, and the ensuing turmoil of the Regency threatened to undermine the very tentative achievement of the Renaissance monarchy and to undo the work of reconstruction accomplished by the first of the Bourbons. Moreover, throughout the sixteenth and seventeenth centuries, the authority of the French crown was tempered, to a greater or lesser degree, by aristocratic power, the self-interest of officeholders, and the great strength of corporate and regional interests generally. Yet during this turbulent era the royal court remained a center of power, of action, and of administrative routine. The continuing vitality of the monarchy and its ability to surmount the Reformation crisis may be explained, in part, by the quality and the durability of the kings' service. Amidst the

3

crises and changes of regimes, the administrative elite remained relatively stable in its composition, and it represented one element of continuity in a government weakened by internal unrest, social conflict, and outright revolution.

Although no single councillor or secretary achieved the reputation of a Sully or the vast powers of a Richelieu, these officers of the crown constituted a corps of highly skilled and loyal servants whose experience and administrative contribution spanned the years of the religious wars and, in certain cases, extended into the first two decades of the seventeenth century. Somewhat in the manner of the modern bureaucrat, the crown servants of the Valois and Bourbon monarchies maintained both a tradition of loyalty and a degree of continuity in operations which were of greatest importance to the functioning of the central power during the long period of crisis. The public careers of Pomponne de Bellièvre and his colleagues suggest that the absolutist state which emerged in the aftermath of the great civil wars was not simply the construction of the cardinal ministers but also the work of men of lesser renown whose power, prestige, and fortunes were closely bound to the development of a strong monarchy.

The public lives of the high administrators of Henry IV centered around three principal institutions—the *Conseil d'état et des finances,* the royal secretariat, and the *Conseil d'affaires.* The *Conseil d'état,* over which the chancellor presided, was charged with the responsibility of directing the king's affairs in "all matters concerning his finances, the peace, care and conservation of his provinces." [1] By the end of the sixteenth century, this body was dominated by administrative experts—intendants of finance and members of the judicial order, the *noblesse de robe,* or *robe longue.*[2] These were the royal officials to whom the Duke of Sully contemptuously referred as that "gang of *maîtres des requêtes* and other 'pointed caps' who mob the council and seek to reduce all affairs of state and finance to chicanery." [3] Sully, of course, was neither the first nor the last representa-

1. Roger Doucet, *Les Institutions de la France au XVIe siècle* (Paris, 1948), I, 145.
2. *Ibid.,* p. 139.
3. Quoted in Noël Valois, "Etude historique sur le Conseil du Roi," *Inventaire des arrêts du Conseil d'état, règne de Henri IV,* ed. Noël Valois (Paris, 1886), I, cvii. (Hereafter cited as Valois, *Inventaire.*)

tive of the *noblesse d'épée* to heap scorn upon the men of "lesser birth" who handled the king's business. However, his bitterness points up the fact that there had taken place in the late sixteenth century a decisive displacement of the old nobility from positions of power within the highest councils of the crown.

Something of the nature of this displacement may be gleaned from a list of the councillors present at the meetings of the *Conseil d'état* in 1594.[4] Of the eleven royal officials who attended thirty or more sessions of the council, five were intendants of finance. Among the remainder, we find the presiding officer, Chancellor Cheverny, and two members of the *robe longue,* Pomponne de Bellièvre and Geoffroy Camus. Ten councillors were in attendance between twenty and thirty times. In this group were three intendants of finance and four representatives of the *robe longue.* Thus, during the reign of Henry IV numerical superiority and, to a degree, effective control of the administrative machinery of the central government lay in the hands of men whom the imperious Sully regarded as of lesser birth—men experienced in financial affairs, the law, or both. Head counting, of course, can be misleading. Numerical preponderance within the *Conseil d'état,* which was strictly an administrative body, did not imply commensurate influence with the king. For this reason, the composition of the *Conseil d'affaires*—a small council where advisory and administrative duties were combined—provides better evidence of the displacement of the great nobles from the innermost chambers of the royal government.

From the fourteenth century there had existed within the *Conseil du roi* a select group of intimate advisers of the crown. This council was variously known as the *Conseil secret,* the *Conseil étroit,* or the *Conseil d'affaires.*[5] Historically, the *Conseil d'affaires* had been dominated by the great lords of the kingdom. Under Henry II, for example, Anne de Montmorency, François de Guise, and the Cardinal of Lorraine had been the principal members, while during the brief reign of Francis II the *Conseil d'affaires* had served as an instrument of the Guise family. At the beginning of the religious wars, then, the council stood as a symbol of the power of the overmighty subjects in the affairs of the royal government.

4. Noël Valois, *Le Conseil du Roi* (Paris, 1888), pp. 227–28.
5. Doucet, *Institutions,* I, 140–42; Valois, *Inventaire,* I, xxxviii–xxxix.

With the coming of civil war, the role of the council in matters of state diminished, and the crown entrusted its most important business to more reliable officials and less obtrusive personalities.[6]

Henry IV revived the *Conseil d'affaires,* which under his immediate predecessor had been virtually indistinguishable from the *Conseil d'état.* Henry's council, however, was dominated by members of the *robe longue* and of the royal secretariat. "Neither quality nor favor served to make one a member of his council," wrote the Marquis de Fontenay-Mareuil, "even the princes of the blood not being members of it."[7] Henry IV selected his principal councillors among "men who, because of their age and former positions, understood all kinds of affairs and were, without doubt, as capable as any in the world." The most renowned and, in time, the most influential of these councillors was Maximilien de Béthune, Baron of Rosny and later Duke of Sully. Occasionally present at the early morning sessions of the council was the constable, Henri de Montmorency.[8] Of those who composed the *Conseil d'affaires,* only Sully and Montmorency were members of the *noblesse d'épée.* Among the others were three representatives of the *robe longue*—Pomponne de Bellièvre, Pierre Jeannin, and Nicolas Brulart, Sieur of Sillery. Of equal importance was the secretary of state, Nicolas de Neufville, Sieur of Villeroy, whose term of service to the crown spanned the years 1559 to 1617.[9]

Bellièvre, Jeannin, Brulart de Sillery, Villeroy, and such councillors and secretaries as Guillaume L'Aubespine, Geoffroy Camus, and Pierre Forget de Fresne formed the nucleus of a corps of high administrators and policy advisers comparable in some respects to the *noblesse des grandes fonctions publiques auprès du roi,* which Philippe Sagnac has described in his study of late seventeenth- and early eighteenth-century French so-

6. On the decline of the *Conseil d'affaires,* see N. M. Sutherland, *The French Secretaries of State in the Age of Catherine de Medici* (London, 1962), pp. 39–42.

7. "Mémoires de Messire du Val, Marquis de Fontenay-Mareuil," *Collection complète des mémoires relatifs à l'histoire de France,* ed. M. Petitot (Paris, 1826), Série I, L, 57–58.

8. Doucet, *Institutions,* I, 143.

9. On Villeroy's career until 1588, see Sutherland, *Secretaries of State,* pp. 150–308. Less useful is J. Nouaillac, *Villeroy, secrétaire d'état et ministre de Charles IX, Henri III et Henri IV* (Paris, 1909).

ciety.[10] Like the secretaries of state and ministers of Louis XIV, the leading administrators under Henry IV were drawn from the ranks of urban notables, magistrates, and royal officials. Again, like their late seventeenth-century counterparts, the principal councillors of Henry IV served their apprenticeships in the royal bureaucracy or in the courts of justice. Socially, both groups of crown servants tended to form a caste apart, an elite within the larger fourth estate of officeholders.

Unlike the ministerial or state nobility of Louis XIV, however, the high administrators and councillors of Henry IV exercised their functions within a system which had not yet hardened into bureaucratic absolutism. They were not bureau chiefs, but rather the personal instruments of the crown who alternately served as advisers, administrators, *commissaires,* and diplomats. In this they were typical representatives of what Roland Mousnier has called the second stage of absolutism—"that of cabinet government with secretaries of state and administrative colleges."[11] Under Henry IV, the crown servants exercised collegial responsibility over a wide range of affairs. The close identification of Sully with the policies of the King, however, has tended to obscure both the fame and contribution of the *noblesse des grandes fonctions* in the age of Henry IV.

II

WITH THE EXCEPTION of such striking figures as the Duke of Sully, crown servants, like modern civil servants, were characterized by a certain anonymity. To treat the high administrators simply as instruments of the crown, however, is to overlook that whole range of private interests, of family and local connections which impinged mightily upon the careers and conduct of all royal agents. If we are to add some flesh to the bare bones of administrative and institutional history, it is to the dynamic and complex society of officeholders that we must turn.[12]

The high administrators and councillors of Henry IV were noblemen

10. *La Formation de la société française moderne* (Paris, 1945), I, 37–38.

11. Fritz Hartung and Roland Mousnier, "Quelques problèmes concernant la monarchie absolue," *Relazioni del X Congresso Internazionale di Scienze Storiche* (Florence, 1955), IV, 29.

12. The fundamental study of the officers is Roland Mousnier, *La Vénalité des offices sous Henri IV et Louis XIII* (Rouen, 1946).

who had, for the most part, familial roots in the bourgeoisie. Their society, however, was separate from both that of the bourgeoisie and that of the *noblesse d'épée*. Like the *noblesse d'épée*, these officers of state possessed landed estates and country houses. Yet ownership of land was in no way central to their power within the royal government or to their prestige within French society. The passage of these officials upward to their high positions in the state was oiled by the wise expenditure of money earned some time in the past in the urban centers of France and by ancestors who were bourgeois. Yet there was nothing specifically bourgeois about their style of life or attitudes. The quality of bourgeois, despite the claims of some historians, was not a genetic inheritance. The single great defining characteristic of this small group of crown servants was that they possessed office and belonged to families which possessed office and enjoyed the spoils of royal patronage. At the height of their careers, these royal officials represented the highest echelon of the fourth estate—an estate which had links with the worlds of commerce, finance, and the landed interests, but which remained a distinct entity within the social and political structures of the French kingdom.

The world of the high officeholders, like that of the *noblesse d'épée*, was characterized by its great families. Nepotism, connections, and family loyalties endowed the fourth estate with its coherence and its hierarchy. It is useful, therefore, if we are to understand the background and setting of the Chancellor's career, to examine the Bellièvre dynasty in the light of the history of other, comparable families.

From what milieu did the great administrative dynasties of the late sixteenth century come? The social origins of these families are often obscured by faulty or fragmentary documentation and by untrustworthy genealogies inserted into the historical record by those eager to suppress evidence of non-noble ancestors. There can be no doubt, however, that the roots of the majority of these families lay in the towns and cities of fifteenth- and early sixteenth-century France. In its close attachment to the municipal and ecclesiastical institutions of Lyons, the Bellièvre clan was typical of the officeholding dynasties of the period. Membership in the governing class of this great intellectual and financial center on the Rhône represented the first stage in the family's rise to political power and social eminence.

8

As is true of so many of the newly ennobled families of the late medieval and early modern eras, the origins of the Bellièvres remain obscure. The researches of Jean Tricou and René Fédou on the legal community in fifteenth-century Lyons have, however, revealed the main lines of the family's early development.[13] The Bellièvres' power in the city was first established by two brothers, Hugonin and Barthélemy, who came to reside in Lyons between 1430 and 1436. The founders of the dynasty were country notaries of modest fortune who formed part of the great wave of immigration to the city during the decade of the 1430's.[14] When he enrolled in the corporation of notaries of Lyons in 1436, Barthélemy I Bellièvre was entitled *clericus de Romenays,* and it would appear that the origins of the family lay in this small town near Besançon.[15] While other relations, "honest merchants named Bel,"[16] remained in Romenay, the principal branch of the family throve in the greater world of Lyons, acquiring offices, prebends, and property at a prodigious rate.

For the Bellièvres, the corporation of notaries, the bureaucracy of the Church, and the *Consulat,* or municipal council, of Lyons served as the institutional bases of family power, fortune, and mobility. Once arrived in the city, the brothers Bellièvre gained a foothold for the family in the corporate life of the legal community and, in time, attached themselves to the court of the archbishopric.[17] Hugonin was a public notary and, between 1443 and 1477, was elected master of the corporation on six occasions. Barthélemy I Bellièvre, from whom the main branch of the family descended, likewise occupied a notarial office and, from 1466, held

13. Jean Tricou's complete genealogy of the family comprises the introduction to Claude Bellièvre, *Souvenirs de voyages en Italie et en Orient, notes historiques, pièces de vers,* ed. Charles Perrat (Geneva, 1956); René Fédou, *Les Hommes de loi lyonnais à la fin du moyen age, étude sur les origines de la classe de robe* (Paris, 1964).

14. Fédou, *Hommes de loi,* pp. 153–78; Abbé Jacques Pernetti, *Recherches pour servir à l'histoire de Lyon: les lyonnais dignes de mémoire* (Lyons, 1757), I, 305–6.

15. Fédou, *Hommes de loi,* p. 145.

16. Claude Bellièvre, *Souvenirs,* p. 28.

17. On the corporation of notaries, see Fédou, *Hommes de loi, passim;* and Jean Déniau, *La Commune de Lyon et la guerre bourguignonne* (Lyons, 1934), pp. 70–72.

9

the position of *procureur général* of the archbishopric.[18] Association with the ecclesiastical establishment of Lyons was clearly decisive in the rise of the Bellièvres, for it brought the clan under the protection and patronage of the Cardinal of Bourbon, Archbishop of Lyons, during the latter half of the fifteenth century.[19] Of equal importance was the connection with the legal profession, which provided the family with access to the *Consulat*.

The interests of the Bellièvres were identified with the legal order at a time when the governing oligarchy of Lyons opened increasingly to representatives of the corporation of notaries. In the fifteenth century the municipal government of Lyons was controlled by a self-perpetuating patriciate, the members of which were drawn from a small number of the city's leading bourgeois families.[20] Actual powers of government, in matters concerning finance and public order, rested in the hands of twelve councillors, who were elected every two years by the masters of corporations. From about mid-century, the *Consulat* underwent an important change in its composition, as the men of the law, including notaries, displaced the older patriciate drawn from the commercial city.[21] By a royal edict issued in 1495, these municipal magistrates of Lyons were granted the juridical status of noblemen—an act which marked the culminating phase in the development of a dynamic and powerful urban elite. Several generations of Bellièvres held seats in the *Consulat,* and thus, from 1495, the family's leading figures enjoyed the personal rank and privileges of the *noblesse de cloche.*

In 1464 Hugonin Bellièvre was elected councillor of Lyons, an office which he occupied on at least four occasions.[22] Henceforth, the Bellièvres joined with like families of lawyers, notaries, and royal officials to form what René Fédou has termed "the government of the legists." [23] Within a span of some sixty years, Bellièvres were elected to the *Consulat* ten times,

18. Bellièvre, *Souvenirs,* pp. ii–iii, v.

19. Abbé Pernetti attributed the rise of the Bellièvres to the protection offered the family by the Cardinal of Bourbon (*Recherches,* I, 306).

20. On the *Consulat,* see A. Kleinclausz, *Histoire de Lyon* (Lyons, 1939), I, 471–73, 492. (Hereafter cited as Kleinclausz, *Lyon.*)

21. Fédou, *Hommes de loi,* pp. 279–92.

22. Bellièvre, *Souvenirs,* pp. ii–iii; Fédou, *Hommes de loi,* pp. 394–95.

23. *Hommes de loi,* p. 375.

and closely related individuals served as councillors until the disappearance of the institution in 1594.[24] Thus, Barthélemy II Bellièvre, who succeeded to his father's offices of public and apostolic notary and secretary of the archbishopric, was twice elected master of the corporation of notaries and occupied a seat on the *Consulat* for five terms between the years 1493 and 1513. In 1523, Claude Bellièvre, son of Barthélemy II and father of the future chancellor, entered the governing council of Lyons and maintained the family's recently acquired status of noblemen.[25]

By the early sixteenth century the Bellièvres were firmly established in the small oligarchy which controlled the municipal government of Lyons; they were on the threshold of the period in which the family's influence was extended beyond its home city and in which its fortunes were tied to the greatest source of patronage in the land, the court of Francis I. Because the Bellièvres were in many respects typical of those families which provided the monarchy with its magistrates and bureaucrats, certain aspects of their rise to power in Lyons deserve emphasis.

First, the Bellièvres were bourgeois of Lyons who rose into the *noblesse de cloche* through municipal officeholding. Yet the phrase "the rising bourgeoisie" tells us virtually nothing about the mechanics of social change or about the dynamics of social mobility in the late fifteenth and early sixteenth centuries. In the earlier, as well as the later, stages of the family's history, the power, prestige, and influence of the Bellièvres were intimately linked to institutions, both ecclesiastical and secular. Patrimonial officeholding, rather than business enterprise, characterized the activities of this bourgeois family. Once acquired, minor offices, professional associations, prebends, and benefices became part of a family legacy, handed down from one generation to the next. The small world of the oligarchs of Lyons was thoroughly imbued with the spirit of a closed corporation.

Initially, as we have seen, the Bellièvres remained bound, both professionally and socially, to the corporation of notaries. Of the four children of Hugonin Bellièvre, for example, one son followed his father as a notary and as master of the corporation, and two daughters married notaries. Among the immediate descendants of Barthélemy I Bellièvre, a

24. "Armorial consulaire de la ville de Lyon," B.N., Ms. fr. 8714, fols. 8–110.
25. Bellièvre, *Souvenirs*, pp. vii, 29; B.N., Ms. fr. 8714, fols. 33, 38.

similar pattern may be observed.[26] The corporation of notaries served the family as one base of power; the Church provided yet another. The office of secretary of the archbishopric, occupied by the first two Barthélemy Bellièvres, became virtually a family possession when, in 1506, Archbishop François de Rohan granted Claude Bellièvre rights of inheritance to the position.[27] Equally striking was the control of canonicates in the collegiate churches of Saint-Just and Saint-Paul exercised by four generations of the family's younger sons. From 1460 until the early sixteenth century, at least ten Bellièvres were received into the confraternities of canons, and canonicates were treated as a form of family property.[28] Through the device of reversions, the Bellièvres, over a period of generations, retained within their patrimony both secretaryships and ecclesiastical prebends.

The rise of the Bellièvres from clerks of Romenay to servants of the crown took place within the framework of the traditional corporate institutions of Lyons. Only one or two generations removed from the country, the early Bellièvres were city men who converted the profits from their legal offices into extensive property holdings in Lyons and the surrounding villages.[29] Whatever their social rank—bourgeois or noble —the family founders were, above all, scribes and legists whose ambitions and acquisitiveness found satisfaction and scope in the legal community of Lyons and in the patronage of the Church.

Service in the bureaucracy of the archbishopric, elective office in the corporation of notaries, and, finally, membership in the *Consulat* combined to form one source of the Bellièvres' local power; landed property comprised yet another. This power, in turn, was solidified by a series of increasingly illustrious marriages into families of newly ennobled magistrates and urban officials of Lyonnais and Dauphiné. By the early sixteenth century, the Bellièvres and their familial connections—the Du

26. Bellièvre, *Souvenirs*, pp. iv–vi, viii.
27. B.N., Ms. fr. 5124, fol. 34.
28. Bellièvre, *Souvenirs*, pp. v, viii–ix, xiv; Maurice Pallasse, *La Sénéchaussée et siège présidial de Lyon pendant les guerres de religion* (Lyons, 1943), p. 139.
29. On the property holdings of the Bellièvres and the growth of these holdings during the fifteenth century, see the wills of Hugonin, Barthélemy I, and Barthélemy II Bellièvre, conveniently reproduced in Fédou, *Hommes de loi*, pp. 464–66, 475–76.

Blets, Fourniers, Langes, and Fayes—composed a powerful and wealthy dynasty of officers and municipal officials typical of those family groupings which came to dominate the royal judiciary and bureaucracy during the *ancien régime.*[30]

Municipal officeholding provided the Bellièvres with their first claim to nobility. Association with that circle of classicists, amateur historians, and collectors of antiquities which promoted humanistic scholarship in Lyons served to endow the family with another sort of nobility—that accorded to the Renaissance gentleman.[31] All of the leading members of the family combined legal training with enthusiastic antiquarianism. Steeped in the sterile humanism of Renaissance France, the Bellièvres collected books, paid for the translation and copying of classical works, and were patrons of Lyons' collection of antiquities.[32] The most notable of the family's scholars was Claude Bellièvre, who was the friend and correspondent of the city's principal humanists, the author of several manuscripts on the history of Lyons, and an amateur classicist.[33] Educated at the universities of Pavia and Turin, the father of the future chancellor held the degree of Doctor of Laws and spent his early years pursuing historical and classical studies.[34] When, in 1531, Claude Bellièvre entered the service of the crown, he stood as the inheritor of a family legacy composed not only of wealth, political power, and connections, but also of a tradition of learning. This is a factor of vital importance in any assessment of the qualities of the men who participated in the great grab for offices which marked the reign of Francis I.

The Bellièvres were, then, a family of substance and considerable

30. On the marriage alliances of the Bellièvres, see Bellièvre, *Souvenirs,* pp. x, 37, 95.

31. This circle is discussed in Mathieu Varille, *Les Antiquaires lyonnais de la renaissance* (Lyons, 1924). Also see Charles Perrat, "Les Humanistes amateurs de papyrus," *Bibliothèque de l'école des Chartes,* CIX (1951), 173–92.

32. On the intellectual and cultural life of the Bellièvres, see James B. Wadsworth, *Lyons, 1473–1503: The Beginnings of Cosmopolitanism* (Cambridge, 1962), pp. 18, 31; Bellièvre, *Souvenirs,* pp. viii, 63–78.

33. Charles Perrat, "Claude Bellièvre et Etienne Dolet," *Bibliothèque d'humanisme et renaissance,* IV (1944), 138–43. An excellent short sketch of Claude Bellièvre's place in the intellectual life of Lyons is to be found in Jean Tricou's introduction to the *Souvenirs,* pp. xv–xviii.

34. Bellièvre, *Souvenirs,* pp. 3–16.

accomplishments before their association with the crown and the royal court. Nearly a century had passed between the family's emigration from Romenay and the establishment of their court connection. In that period, three generations of Bellièvres had amassed a fortune, acquired the personal status of nobility, and, of greatest importance, participated in the processes of local government. The histories of other officeholding dynasties indicate that municipal institutions often served as a springboard into the world of the fourth estate, and that many crown servants of "lesser birth" were, in fact, the heirs of a patiently constructed legacy of power and privilege.

Of all the dynasties which dominated the royal administration in the sixteenth century, none was more important than the Neufville-Villeroys, the family of Henry IV's secretary of state. The Neufville-Villeroys represented the classic case of a bourgeois family which progressed, by means of wealth acquired in commerce, from municipal officeholding into the highest echelons of the royal bureaucracy and thence into the *noblesse d'épée*. It appears that during the fourteenth and fifteenth centuries generations of Neufvilles operated a fish business in the old central market of Paris.[35] Between 1429 and 1500, members of the family were elected as municipal magistrates of Paris on six occasions. As the privileges of nobility had been conferred upon the Parisian magistrates by a royal edict of 1371,[36] the Neufvilles, like the Bellièvres, acquired the juridical status of the *noblesse de cloche* before their entry into the service of the crown.

The records concerning other dynasties of royal servants reveal a pattern of development similar in most respects to that found in the histories of the early Bellièvres and Neufvilles. The distant ancestors of Guillaume L'Aubespine were *marchands bourgeois* and lawyers of Orléans, who held municipal offices during the fifteenth and early sixteenth centuries.[37] The great-grandfather of Nicolas Brulart de Sillery, Jean Brulart, was elected a councillor of the city of Paris in 1511. Finally, the

35. Nouaillac, *Villeroy*, pp. 1–2; B.N., PO. 2102, no. 273.
36. Jean-Richard Bloch, *L'Anoblissement en France au temps de François I*er (Paris, 1934), p. 118.
37. Sutherland, *Secretaries of State*, p. 20; B.N., PO. 1659, no. 221.

father of Pierre Jeannin, though an artisan, was a municipal magistrate of Autun.[38] If we are to establish a pattern or "rhythm" for the upward movement of families in the early modern era, it is clearly with the period of municipal officeholding that we must begin. However various the means to power and to noble status, this small sampling of family histories indicates that a strong base in the urban elite of early modern France represented a main road into the greater world of the royal court.

The second stage of the transformation which raised these urban notables into the aristocracy of royal officeholders came with the acquisition of positions in the small bureaucracy of the crown and in the sovereign courts. As one examines the histories of these few families over a period of several generations, two typical patterns of officeholding emerge. The Bellièvres entered the sovereign court at Grenoble and formed a dynasty of magistrates which extended well into the seventeenth century. The Neufvilles and L'Aubespines, on the other hand, secured offices in the *Maison du roi* and established their families' control over positions in the royal secretariat. Neither of these categories was exclusive, however, and it was not uncommon for a single family to place its members in the sovereign courts, the secretariat, and in other administrative bodies. All royal institutions, whatever their function and nature, were colored by the spirit of patrimonial officeholding which characterized the age. Through venality of offices or simple nepotism, families such as the Bellièvres, Neufville-Villeroys, Brularts, and L'Aubespines laid a hereditary claim upon office in the principal institutions of the realm.

Claude Bellièvre was the first of his family to enter the service of the crown. At a time when many of the notables of Lyons looked beyond the city's confines to the prestige and rewards of provincial officeholding, he procured the office of crown lawyer in the *sénéchaussée* of Lyons and the *baillage* of Mâcon. Francis I created this office in 1531, and it is reason-

---

38. The Brularts de Sillery claimed descent from an old noble family of Champagne. Documents more credible than the seventeenth-century histories of the family place the early Brularts among the lawyers and minor functionaries of Paris and the royal court in the late fifteenth century (B.N., PO. 537, no. 711ᵛ). On the Jeannins, see Noël Garnier, "Le Président Jeannin," *Mémoires de la Société Bourguignonne de Géographie et d'Histoire* (Dijon, 1913), XXVIII, 298.

able to assume that the position of *avocat du roi* in Lyons, like similar offices established throughout the kingdom, was purchased by the holder.[39] From 1531, when he took up his duties as crown lawyer, Bellièvre rapidly climbed within the judicial hierarchy. In 1532 he was granted the office of *avocat fiscal* in the sovereign court of Dombes, which the King placed in Lyons. The letters patent issued by the crown indicate that Bellièvre occupied this office concurrently with that of *avocat du roi*.[40] When the office of *procureur général* in the Parlement of Grenoble was vacated in 1535, Bellièvre obtained it from the King. As *procureur général,* he not only represented the crown before the parlement but also acted as a royal agent called upon to deal with such diverse matters as the territorial problem of the Marquisate of Saluces in Piedmont and the provisioning of troops in Dauphiné.[41] After a decade of service to the monarchy in various legal capacities, Claude Bellièvre was rewarded with the office of president in the Parlement of Grenoble, a position which he held until his retirement from public life in 1544 or 1545.[42]

After three generations of municipal officeholding in Lyons, the Bellièvres, in the person of the president of the Parlement of Grenoble, gained entry into the *noblesse de robe* and thus secured the rights to a hereditary, rather than personal, nobility.[43] Through individual merit or, as is more likely, through a combination of merit, local power, and the purchase of offices, Claude Bellièvre raised his branch of the family into the robe at a time when the magistrates were beginning to comprise the most important segment of the aristocracy of officeholders.[44] Henceforth,

39. *Catalogue des actes de François I*[er] (Paris, 1888), II, 108; B.N., Ms. fr. 5124, fol. 37.

40. *Catalogue des actes,* II, 338; B.N., Ms. fr. 5124, fol. 37.

41. *Catalogue des Actes,* IV, 236, 769; Bellièvre, *Souvenirs,* p. xii.

42. *Inventaire sommaire des archives départementales: Isère, série B,* ed. A. Prudhomme (Grenoble, 1884), II, 11.

43. Although Barthélemy II Bellièvre had been a nobleman, owing to his place in the *Consulat,* his son was titled "bourgeois" of Lyons until his accession to municipal office in 1523. After that, Claude Bellièvre was listed as "noble" in the records of the *Consulat* (B.N., Ms. fr. 8714, fols. 33, 38). As a president of parlement, Claude Bellièvre and his descendants were permanently noble (see Bloch, *L'Anoblissement,* pp. 87–88).

44. On this point, see P. Imbart de la Tour, *Les Origines de la réforme,* 2d ed. (Melun, 1948), I, 451.

the source of the family's honors and power lay less in Lyons than in the courts and councils of the monarchy.[45] A decade after Claude Bellièvre resigned his office of first president to return to Lyons and his scholarly avocation, his two sons, Jean and Pomponne, became councillors in the Parlements of Dauphiné and Chambéry respectively.[46] For a century after 1554, the Bellièvres and their closest kin retained tight control over a series of judicial offices. As he rose in the favor of the crown, Pomponne de Bellièvre served as the principal patron and protector of this robe dynasty.

From 1531 the public lives of the Bellièvres revolved around offices in the royal administration, and these offices, in turn, often were treated as a form of private property. In a like manner, the other families under study in this chapter constructed complex, interlocking dynasties of officeholders and turned the royal administrative system into a vast family enterprise.

Early in the sixteenth century, Nicolas I Neufville, great-grandfather of the most distinguished secretary of state of the sixteenth century, secured the office of notary and secretary of the king. In 1514 he acquired the more illustrious office of secretary of finances. Henceforth, successive generations of the family served in the *Maison du roi* and passed on their increasingly important offices from father to son. Family officeholding was not confined to the secretariat, however, and the Neufville-Villeroys provide the historian with an illuminating case study of plural officeholding. Nicolas I Neufville, for example, was, from 1516, a minor functionary in the chancery and later a treasurer of France. In 1521 he purchased the office of clerk in the *Châtelet* of Paris. A year later, the office was granted to the family in perpetuity, on condition that each heir redeem the clerkship by a payment to the crown. The purpose of this favor was to reimburse Neufville for a loan to the monarchy of 50,000 *livres tournois*. Letters of Francis I, issued in 1538, confirmed the sale to Nicolas II

---

45. The family retained, however, its connections with the Church in Lyons. After entering the Parlement of Grenoble, one son of Claude Bellièvre, Jean, obtained from the papal court a benefice in the diocese, the parish of Abresle and Saint-Germain (Bellièvre, *Souvenirs*, p. xiv). The other son, Pomponne, held several benefices in Lyons concurrently with judicial posts in the royal government.

46. B.N., Ms. fr. 9655, fol. 80.

17

Neufville of yet another clerkship in the *prévôté* and *vicomté* of Paris at the price of 30,000 *livres.* The record of officeholding by the Neufville-Villeroys was spectacular even in an age as venal as the sixteenth century.[47]

The L'Aubespines followed the Neufvilles into the royal secretariat, and in time the two families joined to form a powerful and long-lived dynasty of crown servants. The first of the family to enter the *Maison du roi* was Claude II L'Aubespine, the son of a municipal officer of Orléans, who commenced his public career in 1538 as clerk to the secretary of finances and royal councillor, Guillaume Bochetel.[48] The nature of his duties is revealed in an act of Francis I which called for the payment of 104 *livres* to Claude L'Aubespine "for the writing of several letters patent . . . expedited by Guillaume Bochetel. . . ."[49] L'Aubespine rose from a simple scribe to the office of secretary of state through the patronage of his superior, Bochetel, whose daughter he married in 1543. Not the least of the benefits accruing to L'Aubespine from this alliance were the rights of reversion to his father-in-law's office of secretary of finances.[50] Upon the accession of Henry II in 1547, both Bochetel and L'Aubespine were elevated to the newly created offices of secretary of state. At this juncture in the history of the royal secretariat, several of the four offices of secretary of state became part of the patrimony of the family clientele of Guillaume Bochetel. A royal edict of March 1561 decreed that L'Aubespine's office, after his death, would revert to his son.[51] The younger L'Aubespine, however, secured a secretaryship in 1567 upon the death of an uncle, Jacques Bourdin, yet another of Bochetel's sons-in-law.[52] Claude L'Aubespine then obtained from the crown letters granting survival rights to his office to his son-in-law, Nicolas III de Neufville-Villeroy, contemporary and colleague of Pomponne de

47. The history of officeholding by the early Neufville-Villeroys may be traced in the *Catalogue des actes,* I, 2, 260, 307, 398; III, 654, 688; IV, 288; V, 298. Also see, Nouaillac, *Villeroy,* pp. 4–5.
48. Sutherland, *Secretaries of State,* p. 13.
49. *Catalogue des actes,* VIII, 197.
50. Sutherland, *Secretaries of State,* p. 20; *Catalogue des actes,* VIII, 716.
51. Sutherland, *Secretaries of State,* p. 19; B.N., Ms. fr. 4591, fol. 67.
52. Sutherland, *Secretaries of State,* p. 158.

Bellièvre.[53] If we continue through this complex maze of familial office-holding, we find that Villeroy, in turn, passed on his office to Pierre Brulart, the son of Henry IV's councillor, who married Villeroy's grand-daughter in 1605.[54]

Nicolas Brulart de Sillery, like his fellow councillors in the *Conseil d'affaires* of Henry IV, was heir to a long tradition of officeholding. Although the family numbered among its members both bureaucrats and magistrates, the Sillery branch founded its base of power upon offices in the Parlement of Paris. In 1527 Sillery's grandfather, Pierre I Brulart, obtained the rights to one of twenty new offices in the parlement created by Francis I. The following generation, represented by yet another Pierre, continued the tradition of judicial officeholding. In 1554 Henry II named Pierre II Brulart councillor in the Paris Parlement. The status of the family within the hierarchy of magistrates was improved when, in 1567, Sillery's father acquired the office of president of the *Chambre des Enquêtes*. The offices in the parlement secured by Pierre II Brulart became part of the legacy passed on to his son. In 1573 the future councillor of state received the rights to his father's office of lay councillor. To bypass the rule against the simultaneous occupation of offices in the sovereign courts by father and son, the Brularts obtained a special dispensation from Charles IX. Upon the death of Pierre II Brulart in 1584, his son inherited the offices of president in the *Chambre des Enquêtes* and clerical councillor in the parlement.[55] The Brularts de Sillery engaged fully in the venal practices of their acquisitive society and utilized their wealth to gain extraordinary privileges from the crown.

The families of high officeholders in the middle and late sixteenth century were especially favored by the monarchy, but their histories were altogether typical of an age in which public functions took on the coloration of private property and in which the concept of patrimonial officeholding permeated royal institutions at all levels.[56] The status and

53. Nouaillac, *Villeroy*, p. 15.
54. B.N., Cab. H. 69, fol. 24ᵛ.
55. Officeholding by the Brularts may be traced in the following sources: B.N., Cab. H. 69, fols. 20–20ᵛ; Coll. Clair. 754, fols. 344–47.
56. Roland Mousnier has provided many similar case studies (see *La Vénalité*, pp. 58–62, 495–532).

power of these few families depended upon offices, and officeholding, in turn, gave a distinctive character to their style of life. An examination of the changing social status of these officeholders, their wealth, and their interfamily relationships tells us something of the role of offices in the formation of a sixteenth-century elite.

Officeholding in the royal bureaucracy and sovereign courts provided families of the lesser nobility and the bourgeoisie with a means of rising within the social hierarchy. Royal secretaries, for example, attained a degree of nobility equal to that of a baron and enjoyed all the privileges of noblemen, including the right to transfer this status to their heirs. First presidents of parlements and *maîtres des requêtes* were also nobles of the first degree. Other officers, such as councillors in parlement, royal attorneys, and royal treasurers, acquired the full rights of nobility only gradually. Customarily, three generations of a family occupied an office before the rank of nobleman was conferred upon its posterity.[57] In the cases of such families as the Bellièvres and Neufville-Villeroys, offices in the royal government were not the source of a dramatic rise from lowly bourgeois to noblemen; rather, they were the means of effecting subtle changes in the quality and permanency of the families' *noblesse*. The nobility of the L'Aubespines and Pierre Jeannin, on the other hand, appears to have derived directly from officeholding in the royal secretariat and judiciary. Offices, then, served some as steppingstones into the nobility and others as a way of upward mobility within the second estate.

The social benefits of officeholding are obvious; the economic benefits are somewhat more difficult to determine. Although the exploitation of financial offices provided the holders with great riches, offices in the secretariat and judiciary returned a very modest annual income. Certainly salaries from officeholding formed but a small fraction of the total incomes of those families with which we are concerned. Between 1523 and 1537, for example, the Neufville-Villeroys received for their work in the secretariat an annual sum of 423 *livres*. To this was added an allowance of 1,200 *livres*. For a family which commanded the resources to loan the monarchy 50,000 *livres* on one occasion and 20,000 *livres* on another, a salary of 1,623 *livres* was small indeed.[58] As for the magis-

57. Bloch, *L'Anoblissement*, pp. 76–78.
58. *Catalogue des actes*, II, 147, 256, 274, 760; V, 678, 689; VIII, 72, 278.

trates, a councillor in the Parlement of Paris in 1560 drew an annual salary of 600 *livres*. A clerical councillor, such as Pierre II Brulart, received 400 *livres*. In 1563 Pomponne de Bellièvre's office of councillor in the Parlement of Savoy at Chambéry returned the sum of 600 *livres*.[59] As a general rule, offices were not a source of new wealth for these dynasties of crown servants.

Such figures, however, reveal but a small portion of the economic benefits which accrued to the high officeholders. For one thing, offices gave men status, and status in the sixteenth century meant privilege. Those families which attained the rank of noblemen were exempt from many forms of taxation. In addition, plural officeholding was not uncommon among such families as the Villeroys, Brularts, and Bellièvres. Most importantly, the more privileged members of the fourth estate were the beneficiaries of the extravagant patronage of the royal court. Services to the crown were rewarded not by salaries but rather by the rights to exploit the royal treasury, the Church, and the country generally. Francis I, for example, granted Nicolas I de Neufville an income from funds collected by the royal chancelleries.[60] While serving the monarchy as a diplomat in Switzerland, Pomponne de Bellièvre continued to enjoy the profits of a judicial office in Lyons.[61] In 1608 Henry IV presented Nicolas Brulart de Sillery with the proceeds from the sale of a clerkship in the chancery. Later, Sillery received an outright gift of 30,000 *livres*.[62] For those, such as Sillery, who worked their way into the royal council, the rewards were great. In his *Discours apologétique,* Pierre Jeannin reported that Henry IV granted him 8,000 *livres* annually as councillor and added gratuitously a 6,000 *livre* gift. "Only one or two others," wrote Jeannin, "had such a great salary."[63] On another occasion, Henry IV gave Jeannin the rights to the office of president in the Parlement of Dijon, which office the royal councillor promptly sold for 60,000 *livres*.

Examples of royal generosity could be multiplied, but these few cases suggest that if salaries were small, the profits of officeholding were

59. On the salaries of magistrates, see Mousnier, *La Vénalité,* p. 55. Reference to Bellièvre's salary as councillor is to be found in B.N., Ms. fr. 22480, fol. 13.
60. *Catalogue des actes,* I, 2.
61. B.N., Ms. fr. 15890, fol. 102.
62. B.N., Cab. H. 69, fol. 23; PO. 536, no. 268.
63. "Discours apologétique," B.N., Ms. fr. 3712, fols. 47, 48.

enormous.[64] From the royal court flowed a constant stream of favors, gifts, and benefices which conferred tremendous economic advantages upon the upper echelon of the fourth estate. Small wonder then that the court of the monarchy, as the center of patronage, attracted to it many of the most enterprising families in the kingdom.

The fringe benefits of officeholding—privileges and patronage—comprised one major source of new wealth for families of royal bureaucrats and magistrates. Investment in land, particularly noble land, provided certain of these families both with income and a wide range of titles. The Neufvilles acquired the seigniories of Villeroy and Magny, as well as the lands of Chapelle-la-Reine, Hardeville, and Hallincourt, through the advantageous marriage of Nicolas I de Neufville to the daughter of a newly ennobled officer.[65] In 1518 the Neufvilles received the royal land of Chanteloup, near Chartres, in exchange for certain of their properties in the Parisian faubourg of Saint-Honoré.[66] Likewise, the Brularts secured their principal seigniories, Sillery and Puysieux, through a marriage alliance contracted in 1544. During the first decades of the seventeenth century, Puysieux was raised to a *vicomté* and Sillery to a *marquisate*.[67] Claude II L'Aubespine, owner of at least seven estates, purchased his principal land, the seigniory of Chateauneuf-sur-Cher, from a nobleman.[68] The title of Jean de Bellièvre, Sieur of Hautefort, derived from a noble fief obtained from the Count of Clermont in 1567.[69] In the majority of these cases, the acquisition of seigniories followed the granting of offices which endowed the holders with noble status. Offices, not land, were the major instruments of social transformation. Nor did any of these families turn from officeholding to the life of landed gentlemen. A combination of officeholding and landowning, however, prepared the way for the later entry of certain of these families into the *noblesse d'épée*. As economic investments and as symbols of social standing, landed estates

64. It must be noted that the families with which we are dealing were among the most favored in the kingdom, and that their economic histories were not representative of the fourth estate as a whole.

65. Nouaillac, *Villeroy*, p. 5.

66. *Catalogue des actes*, I, 167, 174.

67. B.N., PO. 620, no. 126; PO. 537, no. 711ᵛ.

68. B.N., PO. 1659, no. 221.

69. B.N., Ms. fr. 8514, fol. 1.

22

were avidly sought by the recently ennobled dynasties of crown servants.

The paucity of information on the economic resources of the great officeholding dynasties precludes any exact calculation of their fortunes or of the impact of royal service upon those fortunes. However, some indication of the vast wealth which certain of these families commanded can be found in marriage contracts and wills. When, in 1604, Claude Brulart, the daughter of Nicolas Brulart de Sillery, married the son of Pomponne de Bellièvre, Sillery provided a dowry of 50,000 *livres* and guaranteed his daughter an annual income of 2,000 *livres*. Bellièvre, in turn, promised his son 3,000 *livres* annually and named him heir to properties valued at 120,000 *livres*. Another of Sillery's daughters received 50,000 *livres* at the time of her marriage. In 1611 Villeroy granted his granddaughter 60,000 *livres* on the occasion of her marriage to Pierre III Brulart. Sillery contributed an annual payment of 6,000 *livres* to his son and principal heir. Upon his death in 1624, Sillery left as bequests to his two daughters 30,000 *livres* in capital, *rentes* returning 8,000 *livres* annually, and lands producing an annual income of 8,000 *livres*.[70] The greater part of Sillery's estate, the value of which was not revealed in his will, fell to his son. Even such fragmentary figures suggest fortunes worth, at a minimum, several hundred thousand *livres*. At the very least, the later generations of these families maintained the fortunes acquired before the period of officeholding in royal institutions. Because of their proximity to the court, the Villeroys, Bellièvres, Brularts, L'Aubespines, and like families not only survived the fierce inflation of the sixteenth century but were among those who did well out of the political, social, and economic turmoil of the age.

At the time when the histories of these families converged—that is, during the second half of the sixteenth century—the principal members of the fourth estate possessed many of the attributes and privileges of the *noblesse d'épée*. Over a period of several generations a highly inbred order of crown servants was formed, whose social status was based upon wealth plus the offices and lands which wealth procured. Despite the titles of knight, squire, and baron which abound in the legal documents concerning these families, the administrators and magistrates formed a social grouping quite distinct from the *noblesse d'épée*. The higher nobility

70. B.N., Cab. H. 69, fols. 19, 25, 30.

scorned the so-called *nobles de dignité* and, as was true of Sully, particularly despised the *noblesse de robe*.[71] Not until the seventeenth century do the family records disclose a significant incidence of intermarriage among the leading dynasties of the fourth estate and members of the sword. In turn, although the aristocracy of officeholders always remained open to new men of wealth and talent, there was an obvious tendency among the established families of officers and administrators to close ranks and marry into families of similar social standing and professional associations.

The dynastic marriage principle did not apply simply to princes and their progeny. Together with a variety of forms of nepotism, intermarriage served to strengthen the hold of a closed circle of officeholders upon commanding positions in the royal administration. In other contexts, we have noted a series of alliances which united the families of L'Aubespine and Villeroy, Villeroy and Brulart, Brulart and Bellièvre. Under both Valois and Bourbon, the government of France was indeed a family affair.

By the last decades of the sixteenth century, the Bellièvres, Brularts, L'Aubespines, and Neufville-Villeroys were firmly established in the self-perptuating elite of officeholders and were closely tied to one another through marriages, common interests, and lengthy association in the councils of the monarchy. Juridically and socially, they were noblemen; professionally, they were crown servants.

III

NOTABLE AMONG THOSE whom the Valois monarchy recruited from the fourth estate into the royal councils was the principal subject of this study, Pomponne de Bellièvre. Like his colleagues in the administrative service of the crown, Bellièvre was the heir to a legacy of privilege and preferment. The second son of Claude Bellièvre and Louise Faye, he was born in Lyons in 1529. Only a fragmentary record remains of his early years. A lawyer by training, Bellièvre followed the traditional path of his family and of the Lyonnais jurists to the great centers of legal studies in southern

71. Mousnier, *La Vénalité*, p. 505.

France and Italy—Toulouse and Padua.[72] As was true of his family generally, the younger Bellièvre was an amateur of the classics, and his style and oratory were formed by his humanistic studies. Among his papers has survived a folio of translations from Greek authors, dedicated to Michel de L'Hôpital, which suggests that he had some scholarly and literary pretensions.[73] Following in yet another family tradition, Bellièvre secured at an early age several benefices in the collegiate churches of Lyons and, as late as 1566, continued to possess a canonicate in the church of Saint-Just and the office of titular pastor of Saint-Martin-Lestra.[74] These latter places in the ecclesiastical establishment of Lyons were held concurrently with positions in the judicial and diplomatic service of the crown.[75]

A family heritage of municipal power and patrimonial officeholding established Bellièvre within the orbit of the royal court at the very beginning of his public life. Obviously this heritage was a central factor in the young lawyer's advancement upward into the nobility of high officeholders. The monarchy recruited its servants from those families distinguished, if not by blood, by wealth, local power, and experience in affairs. Of these family attributes, wealth was by no means the least important—indeed, it was the indispensable condition of crown service.

To a monarchy chronically in financial distress, the wealth of the Bellièvres was a valuable asset. For one thing, during the diplomatic career which preceded his elevation to the royal council, Pomponne de Bellièvre could be relied upon to underwrite French missions abroad. Thus, in a letter to Catherine de Medici's adviser, Jean Morvillier, Bellièvre once complained that in twelve years of service to the crown he had not only failed to profit by a single *denier* but also had been forced to

72. For an account of the education of the legal order of Lyons, see Fédou, *Hommes de loi,* pp. 303–8.

73. B.N., Ms. fr. 16519, fols. 1, 37–75.

74. Bellièvre, *Souvenirs,* p. xiv.

75. Before his appointment as councillor of state in 1570, Bellièvre held the following offices: councillor in the Parlement of Chambéry, 1554–62; lieutenant general in the *baillage* of Vermandois, 1562–64; lieutenant general in the *sénéchaussée* of Lyons, 1564–70. In 1576 he was named president of the Parlement of Paris and occupied this office until 1580.

25

draw upon his personal fortune to carry out his duties.[76] The correspondence between the court and Bellièvre also reveals that he had recourse to his connections in the financial circles of Lyons to provide funds for the crown. For example, a letter from Catherine de Medici in February 1566 indicated that Bellièvre was to use his influence with the *grant parti,* comprising the city's most wealthy families, to gain an extension of certain payments to the monarchy.[77] Another of the Queen Mother's letters, written a decade later, mentioned 300,000 *livres* contributed to the royal coffers by "good servants of the crown, your friends." [78] Catherine warmly praised Bellièvre, who had obtained the loan by pledging that contributors would be reimbursed. Again, when the monarchy defaulted on its financial obligations, it frequently fell to Bellièvre to raise the necessary monies. In October 1566, Catherine suggested that he furnish the funds for a company of Swiss troops on his own credit. On another occasion, Bellièvre was asked to find 180,000 *livres* to provide for a contingent of mercenaries.[79] In numerous ways, then, he utilized his own fortune, his influence in Lyons, and his personal credit among bankers to aid the monarchy financially. Whatever the profits of court office, crown service was, intermittently at least, a burden, which was open primarily to those who, like the Bellièvres, had ample personal resources.

In addition to family position and wealth, access to places of influence and power in the royal government required the support and patronage of established courtiers. Moreover, unlike his colleagues Villeroy and the younger L'Aubespines, Bellièvre was not the direct heir to a court position, and his advancement was particularly dependent upon the good offices of a patron. During the 1560's and early 1570's, two men dominated the administrative sector of the court; they were Sébastien L'Aubespine, Bishop of Limoges, and Jean Morvillier, Bishop of Orléans. It was with Morvillier's faction that Bellièvre associated himself when he entered the *Conseil d'état,* and there is good evidence to suggest that Morvillier sponsored the career of the young councillor.

76. B.N., Ms. fr. 15890, fol. 8, Bellièvre to Morvillier, 6 February 1567.
77. *Lettres de Catherine de Médicis,* ed. H. de la Ferrière (Paris, 1909), X, 164.
78. *Ibid.,* V, 197.
79. *Ibid.,* X, 182; *Lettres de Henri III, Roi de France,* ed. Pierre Champion (Paris, 1959), I, 64.

Of the origins and precise nature of this special relationship, very little can be established. We know that both crown servants shared a close connection with the Italian family of Rucelli—a house which enjoyed the patronage and protection of Morvillier—and it was perhaps some such personal tie which linked the two.[80] Bellièvre regarded Morvillier as his "bon père," and others looked upon the elder man as Bellièvre's "great friend and patron." [81] During the long and dreary years of his diplomatic service in Switzerland, Bellièvre turned to Morvillier for the protection of his interests. In February 1567, for example, he wrote Morvillier from Soleure, expressing his gratitude "that it has pleased you to restore me to their majesties' good graces." [82] Again, in 1568, he addressed a long letter to the royal councillor thanking him for his aid in procuring a recompense from the crown.[83] On another occasion, the suggestion was apparently made at court that in Bellièvre's absence his office of *lieutenant général* of the *sénéchaussée* of Lyons should be shared with another officer, for in April 1568, Bellièvre promised lifelong devotion to Morvillier, who had "taken up my protection in order to preserve for me in its entirety the office of *lieutenant général* of Lyons." [84] Six years later, it was Morvillier who assured Bellièvre, at the time ambassador to Poland, that upon his return he would occupy a ranking position in the court of Catherine de Medici.[85] Thus from the period of his diplomatic career to the beginning of his ascendancy in the administrative and political service of the Queen Mother, Bellièvre appears to have been Morvillier's man.

IV

THE PRECEDING SKETCH of the administrative sector of the court and of the family and personal factors involved in Bellièvre's rise to high office forms the essential background to the Chancellor's years of service under the crown. The nonpolitical dimensions of officeholding have been exam-

---

80. Bellièvre mentioned the Rucelli connection in a letter written to his friend Villeroy in March 1598 (B.N., Ms. fr. 15894, fol. 25).
81. B.N., Ms. fr. 15902, fol. 123, Truchon to Bellièvre, April 1572.
82. B.N., Ms. fr. 15890, fol. 8.
83. *Ibid.*, fol. 89, Bellièvre to Morvillier, 22 February 1568.
84. *Ibid.*, fol. 102, Bellièvre to Morvillier, 11 April 1568.
85. B.N., Ms. fr. 15903, fol. 16, Morvillier to Bellièvre, 23 January 1574.

ined to evoke that milieu of family connections, patronage, and corruption within which the king's business was carried forward. There is another side to the story of the great officeholding dynasties, however, and this concerns the functions of the most eminent crown servants at a time when the monarchy was deep in crisis. The great grab for spoils and offices which has been described should not obscure the fact that out of the ranks of lawyers, scribes, magistrates, and placemen there emerged quite a few officers of state who were well suited by training, experience, and even by family tradition to exercise the functions of government. This was certainly true of Bellièvre. For some three decades he stood at the center of power in the kingdom. Over half of these years were passed in the entourage of Catherine de Medici. It was Catherine who made Bellièvre's career, although it was Henry IV with whom that career became indissolubly linked.

In the Service of

Catherine de Medici

IN 1585, WHEN THE FORTUNES of the French monarchy were at low ebb, Sir Edward Stafford, the English ambassador to France, wrote the following of the court of Henry III: "Truly, in my opinion, never King was more betrayed than the French King of them he hath most bound to him, and do not think any true counsellor about him but only Villeroy and Bellièvre."[1] Among those who emerged from the leading officeholding dynasties of the sixteenth century to occupy high positions of state, Villeroy and Bellièvre were pre-eminent. Throughout the long years of political discord and civil strife which marked the reign of Henry III, these two men were the principal servants of the crown and the particular favorites of the Queen Mother, Catherine de Medici.

After the death of Henry II, the task of preserving the monarchy from the incursion of ideology and foreign influence into French politics fell to

1. *Calendar of State Papers, Foreign Series, of the Reign of Elizabeth*, ed. Sophie Crawford Lomas (London, 1916), XIX, 390. (Hereafter cited as *C.S.P., For.*)

his widow, who with great cunning and some courage sought to maintain the crown for her feckless sons. Catherine gathered around her a loyal band of councillors and administrators who served as her principal officials. The dreary story of the Queen Mother's efforts to fend off the factions and save the throne for her children is well known. The men who were instrumental in carrying out her policies, however, have been relatively neglected by historians.[2] Bellièvre filled such a role, and was one of many statesmen of the sixteenth century who learned the art of politics under the tutelage of Catherine de Medici.

II

THE YEARS of Bellièvre's ascendancy at the court of the Queen Mother extended from approximately 1575 until his forced retirement in 1588, and it is upon this period that the following pages focus. First, however, brief consideration must be given to his early service, to his character, and to his thought.

Offices in the judiciary and connections with the notables of officeholding society formed part of Bellièvre's birthright. His selection as councillor of state in 1570, however, did not follow simply from the privileged circumstances of his family. From the time of his entry into the short-lived Parlement of Chambéry in 1554 until his elevation to the royal council, some sixteen years elapsed. The majority of those years were passed in Switzerland, where Bellièvre served a lengthy and frustrating apprenticeship as royal agent and ambassador.

Although he had undertaken two minor missions to Switzerland in 1560 and 1562, Bellièvre's diplomatic service commenced in the spring of 1564, when he was appointed ambassador extraordinary to the cantons and ambassador to the Grisons in the eastern Alps.[3] At the time of his appointment, Bellièvre occupied the office of *lieutenant général* in the

2. On Villeroy's career during this period, see N. M. Sutherland, *The French Secretaries of State in the Age of Catherine de Medici* (London, 1962), *passim*.
3. For a detailed narrative of Bellièvre's Swiss missions, see Edouard Rott, *Histoire de la représentation diplomatique de la France auprès les cantons suisses* (Paris, 1902), II, 12–27, 119–30, 153–59. (Hereafter cited as Rott, *Représentation diplomatique*.)

baillage of Vermandois and, in the first years of the religious wars, was engaged in the pacification of Laon and its region.[4] In March 1564, Catherine de Medici ordered him to settle his affairs and to join the court at Troyes, "Because the King . . . wishes to employ you in something of importance to his service."[5] Shortly thereafter, Bellièvre was dispatched to the cantons to renew the alliance of 1549 between France and the Swiss Leagues.[6] For nearly a decade, he served as the chief representative of the French court in its most important diplomatic mission.

The Swiss missions were of particular significance, in light of Bellièvre's later career, because it was in the cantons that he first entered into the undercover battle against the agents of the Spanish monarchy. His initial assignment, as explained in letters of Charles IX, was "to straighten out what the ambassador of the Catholic King . . . has tried to confuse" and to prevent an alliance between Spain and the Grisons.[7] This was doubly difficult because, as Bellièvre informed Morvillier, the Swiss were a people "who do not know what it is to have a war in their house,"[8] and because French diplomacy was inadequately financed. Diplomacy in Switzerland consisted, in large part at least, of persuasion backed by bribery, and Bellièvre complained incessantly that "I spend an unbelievable amount here, so that I shall soon be without money."[9] Despite the frustrations of his mission, the Ambassador maintained the alliance, annually raised contingents of mercenaries for the crown, and above all checked Spanish designs to remove the cantons from the French sphere of influence.[10]

For his loyal service, Bellièvre received both praise and rewards from the court. On two occasions in 1568, Catherine wrote to him with promises of patronage and future promotions. In one letter she assured

4. B.N., Ms. fr. 15901, fol. 1, Montmorency to Bellièvre, March 1563; fol. 2, Catherine de Medici to Bellièvre, March 1563.
5. B.N., Ms. fr. 16013, fol. 2, Catherine de Medici to Bellièvre, March 1564.
6. *Ibid.,* fol. 4, Charles IX to the Swiss cantons, May 1564.
7. *Ibid.,* fol. 9, Charles IX to Bellièvre, 28 May 1564; fol. 15, Charles IX to Bellièvre, June 1564.
8. B.N., Ms. fr. 15909, fol. 81, Bellièvre to Morvillier, 16 February 1568.
9. B.N., Ms. fr. 16014, fol. 29, Bellièvre to *Conseil d'état,* January 1565.
10. Rott, *Représentation diplomatique,* II, 119–30.

Bellièvre that "The services which you perform continually for the King
. . . are so pleasing to him and to me . . . that the office of President of
Lyons, which he formerly gave you, is the least of the rewards which he
wishes to grant for your services." [11] Two years later, in July 1570,
Bellièvre was granted the supreme reward for his apprenticeship in
Switzerland—promotion to the royal council.

Elevation to the council did not, however, terminate Bellièvre's diplomatic role in the cantons. Among the first of many conciliatory missions
which he undertook between 1570 and 1588 was a journey to Baden, in
December 1572, where he explained and defended the violent massacre
of Saint Bartholomew's Day. Before the representatives of the Protestant
regions assembled at the Diet of Baden, Bellièvre argued that Admiral
Coligny had desired to introduce a "dangerous tyranny" in France, and
that consequently the massacre was not a reprisal against the Huguenots
but rather a measure of self-protection taken against rebellious subjects.
Although he expressed regret at the bloodshed which followed the assassination of Coligny, Bellièvre contended that the issue at stake was nothing
less than the conservation of the crown, and that the King and Catherine
had dealt justly with the threat.[12] When Huguenot refugees visited him in
Baden, he wrote Charles IX, "I told them . . . that they could well judge
that this division of opinions had led them to sedition." [13] Bellièvre's
defense of the crown aroused religious passions in Switzerland, but the
Protestant cantons remained loyal to the French monarchy and allowed
him to raise a troop of 6,000 soldiers for service in Burgundy.[14] As
ambassador extraordinary, the royal councillor had partially redressed the
damage caused by the bloody events of August 1572 and had skillfully
calmed the fears of those who, after Saint Bartholomew's Day, anticipated
a Catholic crusade to impose the decrees of the Council of Trent upon
Europe.[15]

11. *Lettres de Catherine de Médicis,* ed. Count Baguenault de Puchesse (Paris,
1909), X, 244, 250. (Hereafter cited as *Lettres Médicis.*)

12. B.N., Ms. fr. 15895, fols. 17–41.

13. B.N., Ms. fr. 15890, fol. 241, Bellièvre to Charles IX, 11 March 1573.

14. Rott, *Représentation diplomatique,* II, 167; B.N., Ms. fr. 15890, fol. 219ᵛ,
Bellièvre to Charles IX, January 1573.

15. B.N., Ms. fr. 15890, fol. 212ᵛ, Bellièvre to Charles IX, 15 December
1572.

III

BELLIÈVRE REMAINED IN SWITZERLAND until the late spring of 1573, when the negotiations concerning the Swiss mercenaries were completed. Upon his return to France, he became deeply involved in Catherine's attempts to pacify the country and to solve politically those problems of state which massacre had only aggravated. To meet the crisis created by the factions, the Queen Mother fashioned her own clientele from within the court and depended upon her administrative experts, the secretaries and *gens de robe,* to implement policies designed to protect the sovereign rights of her sons. By the early 1570's, Bellièvre was firmly established in that small circle of loyalists upon whom Catherine relied, and he proved to be an excellent instrument of her politics, which combined maternalism and Machiavellism in equal measure.

Poised between the clashing factions, Catherine and her creatures were, out of necessity or conviction, political moderates. Like his patroness, Bellièvre understood that legitimacy and loyalty had to be placed above all other considerations if the state were to survive. Indeed, Bellièvre was singularly equipped, both by character and training, to serve the purposes of the Queen Mother. He was, in Stafford's estimation, "a good and wise counsellor for the state, which he loveth; politic and wise." [16] Cautious and temperate, Bellièvre displayed in his public life both the virtues and the limitations of the political moderate. Having risen to power in an age which seemed to him dominated by immoderate passions, the royal councillor claimed that his spirit "conformed to the rules of reason rather than to those of passion." In truth, Bellièvre's personality and ideas were generally overshadowed by those whose instrument he was. When in 1584 the English ambassador, seeking France's aid in the struggle against Spain, approached him, Bellièvre was forced to voice his master's opposition. "The tears ran down his cheeks," Stafford wrote to Walsingham, "and he told me that there was no remedy for servants, but when they had declared their consciences to their Masters, to declare their Masters' minds as they gave him commandment." [17] It is, then, the relative impersonality

16. *C.S.P., For.,* XVIII, 621.
17. *Ibid.*

33

of the crown servant, revealed in this minor incident, which characterized Bellièvre's image in the sixteenth century. As a conciliator, loyalist, and man of commonsensical reason, he left a very different imprint upon his times than did those overmighty subjects who were the principal objects of his diplomacy and political activities.

To his political role under the last Valois monarchs, Bellièvre brought a public philosophy shaped by his loyalties to the crown, to the Roman Church, and to his order, the *robe longue.* He was both a Catholic, who longed for the restoration of a united Christendom, and a *politique,* who rejected force as a solution to the Reformation crisis. These two not entirely consistent aspects of his thought were best expressed in a short, undated essay entitled "On the Divisions of Christianity." [18]

In this essay, Bellièvre set forth in broad outlines the political notions of the loyalist party, the court *politiques.* Civil war over religion, he warned, threatened the very existence of the Catholic Church in France. To those who desired to resolve the religious question through militancy, Bellièvre responded by citing the history of the civil war in France and of the struggle in the Low Countries between Spain and her rebellious Protestant subjects. These events demonstrated that bloodshed in the name of religion only served to diminish the power and prestige of the true Church. Bellièvre advocated the withdrawal of the state from the religious conflict between Catholic and Calvinist. "The cause of the faith must be upheld by bishops and prelates," he wrote, "and not by secular judges who have tried to expel the new religion by force from the kingdoms of England, Denmark, Sweden, and Scotland." The fight against Protestantism was to be waged with "one's head rather than with one's arms." Both the survival of the Roman Church and reasons of state dictated a pacific resolution to the religious crisis.

From his analysis of the effects of the religious wars, Bellièvre turned to the preservation of Christian unity and the achievement of the "universal reunion" of Christian states. It is in this portion of his essay that one can discern both the lingering nostalgia for an idealized Christian republic of states, which characterized one strain of Bellièvre's political thought, and his keen understanding that the early modern European

18. B.N., Ms. fr. 15892, fols. 10–16.

state was fundamentally an instrument of aggression. To overcome the divisions of Christendom, the crown councillor proposed a holy war against the Turks. "It is not possible to preserve the domestic peace," he wrote, "except by a foreign war. It appears necessary that all Christian potentates, of both religions, undertake as fellow citizens to make war upon the Mohammedans." The states of Europe, Bellièvre suggested in a vivid analogy, were like stomachs which, "if they do not digest some substance given them for the nourishment of the body . . . attract and consume the substance of the body." The Christian Commonwealth, then, was to be nourished on a diet of infidels. Through a Christian crusade, the self-interest of all parties was to be satisfied. The power of the papacy would be enhanced by the support of all Christians and peace would be restored to the Empire. Above all, the monarchy of France would be preserved and the way prepared for the integration of all dissident subjects into the state. "The King of France," wrote Bellièvre, "would enjoy peace in his kingdom, and through his prudence and authority he would order his affairs in such a manner that the Catholics would be gladdened, and the remainder of his subjects would, in the end, follow the example . . . of their good King." The unification of Christianity through a crusade against the Turks was less an end in itself than a means to the reconstruction of the French kingdom.

However simplistic in parts, "On the Divisions of Christianity" contained the rudiments of the political philosophy which Bellièvre would develop more fully during the later phase of the religious wars. In it, nostalgia for the shattered Christian Commonwealth was tempered by a diplomat's appreciation of the interests of states and an understanding of the violence which underlay his society. Ultimately, it was the French state, not the Christian Commonwealth, which was the higher object of Bellièvre's loyalty. In the tradition of the *légistes,* who over the centuries had elaborated the theoretical structure upon which monarchical power was based, Bellièvre staunchly upheld the sovereign rights of the crown. The good state which he envisioned was one in which the king acted as the common father of his people and in which the law prevailed over the wills of men and tempered royal authority by justice. When the Edict of Boulogne of 1573 offered a brief hope of respite from civil war, Bellièvre

35

put forward in a memorandum to the King his ideas on the reconstruction of the kingdom.[19]

The fundamental problem confronting the monarchy, Bellièvre suggested to the King, was the continuing mistrust which existed in the "hearts of your subjects who have followed or remain of the new opinion." To overcome the fears of the Protestants, the King was to serve as the "common father" of his subjects, applying the law equally to all and punishing those who contravened the edicts of toleration. In addition, the times demanded a complete reformation of customs to cleanse the state of corruption and of the defiance introduced by the religious wars. The foundations of a healthy society, Bellièvre stated, were the sound instruction of youth, good laws, and the appointment of uncorrupt magistrates. He particularly emphasized the need to reform the judiciary. Because justice stood as the mainstay of royal power, the councillor called for extraordinary measures to purge the courts and to reduce the number of officers. "Knowing that evil in the kingdom has come about and continues principally through the fault of the officers," Bellièvre wrote, "it is a question of putting men of good will in the place of bad ones." Loyalists were to be dispatched throughout the kingdom to hear the complaints of the crown's subjects and to punish disloyal officers. Lawgiving, he argued, represented "the highest and most excellent gift" which God bestowed upon kings. The re-establishment of what the councillor called "the French republic" depended upon the reformation of the judicial system.

The political necessity of toleration, the primacy of law, and the restoration of public morality through judicial reform remained constant themes in the political discourses of Bellièvre. His vision of the good state included an important place for the established families of the *robe longue,* which would serve as one of the pillars of a paternalistic monarchy. The nobles of the sword, in turn, "were born to beat down the pride of foreigners" and not to make war upon the crown. One may presume that the crusade against the Turks, advocated by Bellièvre, was among other things a device to distract the sword and to keep order in the kingdom.

Amidst the bloodletting and corruption of the sixteenth century,

19. B.N., Ms. fr. 15890, fols. 387–89.

Bellièvre looked back to an age which he thought more virtuous, to a society in which the orders were fixed in their relations with the crown, and to a kingdom patterned, in good humanistic fashion, upon an idealized Roman Republic. The course of events, however, shattered the councillor's hopes for the unification of Christendom, internal peace, and the reformation of customs. He was drawn into the arena of political strife, where as an emissary of the Queen Mother he assumed the role of conciliator and peacemaker.

IV

As *conseiller d'état et privé,* Bellièvre performed a variety of functions for the crown. For some eight years he filled the office of superintendent of finances, and throughout his councillorship he exercised a general direction over the monarchy's fiscal affairs.[20] In these years of breakdown and civil war, however, administration was necessarily subordinated to politics, and it was as a political agent of Catherine de Medici that Bellièvre played his most important role. From the viewpoint of the court, high politics were to a remarkable degree family politics. Major issues of war and peace, foreign relations, and religious controversy often took the very personal form of quarrels within the royal family or between the crown and related clans. Thus Bellièvre's service to the Queen Mother may be explained in large part through his relationships with the notables of the realm. He was Catherine's appointed watchdog over her sons, her principal representative to the court of Henry of Navarre, and, in the late 1580's, the chief intermediary between the throne and the house of Guise-Lorraine.

Within months of returning from his final diplomatic mission to the Swiss, Bellièvre was appointed ambassador to the newly elected King of Poland, the future Henry III. Although Charles IX's edict of December 1573 stated only that Bellièvre should serve as ambassador and conclude

20. Between 1571 and 1574, Bellièvre, along with such experienced councillors as Morvillier and Sébastien L'Aubespine, served in the *Conseil des finances.* Henry III suppressed this council in 1574 and appointed Bellièvre superintendent of finances. In 1582, when the King revived the *Conseil des finances,* Bellièvre joined with eleven other crown servants to exercise a collective control over finances.

a treaty of alliance between France and Poland, he was in fact Catherine's personal agent at her son's court.[21] Catherine carried on an intimate correspondence with the Ambassador concerning Henry's education, moods, and marriage prospects.[22] Like his royal charge, Bellièvre found his brief sojourn in Poland a period of unhappy exile. He wrote to Morvillier deploring the kingdom's precarious financial situation and incommodities: "The revenues are so reduced that we do not know how we are to govern."[23] The Polish interlude quickly ended with the death of Charles IX in May 1574. Toward the middle of June, Bellièvre formed an advance party which preceded the new King of France in his secret, nocturnal flight from Cracow and then accompanied the monarch homeward to a France as ungovernable as the poor and backward kingdom of Poland.

The immediate cause of the crisis facing the young King in the first years of his reign was the alliance of Huguenots and "malcontents" led by Catherine's favorite son, the Duke of Anjou. Against the crown stood the factions of Anjou, the Prince of Condé, and Henry of Montmorency-Damville, supported by the German mercenaries of Duke Casimir of the Palatinate.[24] To break the alliance and rid France of German reiters, Bellièvre undertook several missions between January and July of 1576. In order to deal with Casimir, the Queen Mother had written Morvillier, a man of intelligence and fidelity was required. "I say that Bellièvre is necessary," she continued, "and tell this to the King for me."[25] No set of negotiations better illustrated the fundamental weaknesses of the monarchy or the frustrations of the peacemakers at court. Of Condé and Casimir, Bellièvre complained, "They are armed and we speak barehanded. This means that our words, even when they come from the

21. This point is made by Louis Monnier in his "Les Missions diplomatiques de Pomponne de Bellièvre," *Ecole Nationale des Chartes, positions des thèses* (Paris, 1930), p. 120. (Hereafter cited as Monnier, *Missions*.)

22. B.N., Ms. fr. 15903, fols. 34, 40, Catherine de Medici to Bellièvre, April 1574.

23. B.N., Ms. fr. 15890, fol. 334, Bellièvre to Morvillier, 16 March 1574.

24. For Bellièvre's account of the links between the factions, see B.N., Cinq Cents de Colbert, 8, fol. 20, Bellièvre to the Duke of Mayenne, 16 January 1576.

25. *Lettres Médicis,* V (1895), 310.

mouth of the Master himself, have little effect." [26] So little effect, indeed, that the royal emissary ended his mission as a prisoner of Duke Casimir.

At issue in the negotiations were the presence of German troops in France, Casimir's demand of payments, and the uncertain ambitions of the Duke of Anjou. The Huguenot leaders, Bellièvre reported to the King, encouraged the impetuous Duke in his designs upon Flanders.[27] Under such conditions the crown had but one recourse—massive bribery. Toward the beginning of Bellièvre's mission, Gaspard de Schomberg had written the King from Nancy, "Bellièvre has his passport to go to Monsieur the Prince of Condé. . . . There can be no doubt that their demands will be high and great, but from what I have learned, you can get out of everything with money." [28] In fact, concessions on matters of religion were required as well. After the failure of Bellièvre's preliminary negotiations, Henry III and his mother granted the Protestants extensive rights of worship and protection, along with bribes, under the terms of the Peace of Monsieur of May 1576. The monarchy had not, however, the resources to meet its obligations.

In June, Bellièvre went to Andelot and sought to calm Casimir and his colonels, who were enraged because "I had come without bringing them money, or certitude of the sum which they will receive, or of the time." Without money, Bellièvre warned the King and Catherine, he could not implement the peace. "If I had the means to enter into negotiations," he wrote, "it is certain that Monsieur, your brother, would tomorrow say farewell to Casimir and make his way toward Bourges." [29] Following Bellièvre's pleas, the crown did grant Casimir partial payment in cash and goods, but the completion of negotiations foundered on the question of French hostages to guarantee a final settlement.[30] Ignoring diplomatic convention, Casimir took Bellièvre prisoner in August, and the royal councillor remained a hostage until his release at Heidelberg the next month. With the help of the good offices of the Count Palatine, an

---

26. B.N., Cinq Cents de Colbert, 8, fol. 20.
27. *Ibid.*, fol. 18, Bellièvre to Henry III, 17 June 1576.
28. *Ibid.*, fol. 5, Schomberg to Henry III, 2 January 1576.
29. *Ibid.*, fol. 150, Bellièvre to Henry III, 17 June 1576.
30. B.N., Fonds Dupuy 502, fol. 118ᵛ, Henry III to Casimir, n.d.

agreement was reached by which Bellièvre promised to deliver hostages to Casimir, and the Duke in turn offered safe-conduct to future emissaries of the French crown.[31]

Despite the humiliating outcome of his negotiations with Duke Casimir, Bellièvre continued to enjoy the full confidence of the Queen Mother, who entrusted him with the most delicate affairs of state. Inevitably, such affairs involved the most venturesome of her brood, the Duke of Anjou. The embroglio with the Huguenots and Casimir in 1576 had demonstrated the Duke's potential powers as a leader of the dissidents, and until his death in 1584 he posed a threat to the internal peace of the kingdom and to its relations with Spain. In Flanders, Anjou pursued his private foreign policy; at home he attempted to extend his personal dominion.

During the summer of 1578, Bellièvre went to the Low Countries to deter the Duke from his plan to conquer the Spanish provinces—a scheme which the crown opposed for fear that in the midst of France's civil strife Anjou might provoke an open conflict with Philip II.[32] To forestall an alliance of Anjou and the rebellious Estates General of the Low Countries, the royal councillor offered the good offices of his King as a means of ending the war with Spain.[33] By a treaty ratified on August 20, however, the Estates designated Anjou "Defender of the liberty of the Low Countries against the tyranny of the Spaniards," thereby undermining Bellièvre's efforts to repair France's relations with the Spanish monarchy.[34] Upon his return from the Low Countries, Anjou once again defied his brother by forming a personal clientele among the officers and members of the Estates of Normandy. In March 1579 Bellièvre was sent to Caen, where he sought to reconcile the Duke with Henry III and to break up the Norman League.[35] On this occasion Catherine expressed her confidence in the diplomatic prowess of Bellièvre. "I am pleased that you have sent to your brother," she wrote the King, "and that you have chosen the

31. *Ibid.*, fols. 121, 123–29.

32. Monnier, *Missions*, pp. 121–22; *Lettres Médicis*, VI, 22.

33. B.N., Ms. fr. 15891, fols. 3–4ᵛ.

34. *Actes des Etats Généraux des Pays-Bas, 1576–1585*, ed. M. Gachard (Brussels, 1861), I, 408, 413–15.

35. B.N., Ms. fr. 15891, fols. 35–36, Bellièvre to Henry III, 10 May 1579; *Lettres Médicis*, VI, 159, 209.

sieur de Bellièvre. . . . As he is a lover of peace and a loyal and devoted servant, I do not doubt but that he will accomplish a great deal." [36] The homilies of the crown servant failed to move Anjou, who refused to dismantle his league until all such associations were disbanded by order of the King. Bellièvre, in turn, proposed to Henry III that a pension, derived from the tax revenues of Tours and Berry, be offered in order to restrain the Duke's political activities. Otherwise, he warned, Anjou would be tempted "to put his hands on the funds from your *tailles*." [37] In the end, bribery succeeded in detaching the King's brother from the opposition, and he joined with Bellièvre and Villeroy in the negotiation of the Peace of Fleix of November 1580.

The frustrating work of peacemaking that was undertaken by Catherine and her servants met with a very temporary and partial success at Fleix. There the so-called Lovers' War, which had been waged in the south between the forces of Henry of Navarre and those of Maréchal Biron, was settled. After a month of negotiations, during which Villeroy and Bellièvre served as honest brokers, the contending factions agreed to a truce and the Protestants were allowed to retain their fortified places in the southwest for a limited period of time.[38] Upon the conclusion of the Peace of Fleix, Catherine ordered Bellièvre to remain in Guienne to oversee both the execution of the treaty and the activities of the Duke of Anjou, who contemplated further adventures in the Low Countries. The peace achieved by the crown servants was short-lived, as was the cooperative temper of Anjou.

By the late 1570's, indeed before, the religious component of the civil wars was overshadowed by the ambitions and personal rivalries of the factions and their leaders. The south and the southwest were the particular preserves of the overmighty subjects, and there Bellièvre passed the greater part of his service between 1580 and 1585. To the royal councillor, engaged in the fruitless task of reconciling the warring groups, the collapse of the Valois monarchy appeared imminent. From Fleix,

36. *Lettres Médicis*, VI, 303.
37. B.N., Ms. fr. 15891, fol. 35ᵛ.
38. For a recent statement on the Peace of Fleix, see Sutherland, *Secretaries of State*, pp. 213–14. Bellièvre's reports on the peacemaking are to be found in *Lettres Médicis*, VII, 451–53.

Bellièvre had addressed a grim report to Henry III, describing the corruption and disorder which beset the provinces.[39] Some five years later, when the optimism generated by the Peace of Fleix had long since disappeared, he wrote Catherine from Paris, "We are doing what we can here, but the more I think about it, the more I judge this miserable kingdom to be near its end if God will not permit this upheaval to end soon." [40]

Bellièvre's pessimism stemmed from a succession of failures in his negotiations with Anjou, Navarre, Condé, and the lesser Huguenot leadership. The primary objectives of his missions in the southwest were to secure from Henry of Navarre the surrender of certain fortified places and to keep close watch upon the Duke of Anjou. Of his future master, Navarre, the royal councillor wrote, "It will be very difficult to cleanse his mind of the many suspicions implanted in this atmosphere of civil war." [41] Anjou, in turn, he found tired and bored by protracted negotiations and eager to satisfy his honor in the Low Countries. From the various proposals for internal peace which were put to Bellièvre by Anjou and the others, one can sense the heated and impossible political conditions under which the crown servants worked. When, for example, Bellièvre urged the Duke to forget his designs upon Flanders, the latter replied that he would cleanse the kingdom of dissidents by taking them with him to the Low Countries.[42] The Queen of Navarre hatched yet another scheme. If her husband remained in Guienne, she told Bellièvre, disorders would continue "unless the King finds the means to occupy him." Her solution was outlined by Bellièvre in a letter to Villeroy: "She judges that if the King wants to employ him in the enterprise for the recovery of the Kingdom of Portugal, her husband will gladly accept the charge because of his desire to prove his worth." [43] In this environment colored by aristocratic pride and intrigue, Bellièvre endeavored to enforce the provisions of the treaty made at Fleix. To Catherine he wrote, "If I am not

39. B.N., Ms. fr. 15891, fol. 74, Bellièvre to Henry III, 22 November 1580.
40. *Ibid.*, fol. 389, Bellièvre to Catherine de Medici, 3 April 1585.
41. *Lettres Médicis*, VII, 471.
42. B.N., Ms. fr. 15891, fol. 104, Bellièvre to Catherine de Medici, 31 December 1580.
43. *Ibid.*, fol. 207, Bellièvre to Villeroy, 6 April 1581.

deceived this is one of the most difficult affairs ever treated in the kingdom, and I confess the charge surpasses my strength."[44]

Throughout the year 1581, Bellièvre labored to separate Navarre from his Protestant clientele in Guienne, Languedoc, and Dauphiné. Although Henry agreed in general terms to support the edicts of peace and restrained such firebrands as Condé, he refused to abandon "those of Dauphiné who have taken his side." He insisted, moreover, as a condition for his cooperation, that certain of his properties occupied by royalist forces be restituted. Bellièvre urged the King to satisfy his cousin on this point, but he warned that "The King of Navarre is so bound to those of Dauphiné, and also to those of Languedoc and Guienne, who profess this religion, that even though they have given me all the promises and oaths in the world, I cannot believe them."[45]

The Duke of Anjou was, if anything, less tractable and less open to the royal councillor's diplomatic wiles. A month after the Peace of Fleix, Bellièvre informed Catherine that the Duke spoke ever more passionately of his affairs in Flanders and complained that his honor was sacrificed to the advantage of Philip II.[46] Bellièvre had responded that the crown would assist Anjou in the Low Countries once internal order was achieved, but the Duke pursued his independent course by recruiting both Navarre and Biron for his enterprise.[47] This alliance of former antagonists proved to be ephemeral, but in May Anjou escaped the royal councillor's surveillance, "gave in to his passion," and set out for Flanders. In September 1581, Henry III sent Bellièvre to the Prince of Parma in another unsuccessful attempt to mediate the dispute between Spain and its rebellious provinces.[48] The crisis in France's foreign relations continued to be aggravated by the rupture within Catherine's disputatious family.

As the principal royal agent in the south, Bellièvre also had to deal with the shock troops of rebellion—the lesser nobility, urban officials, and

44. *Ibid.,* fol. 153, Bellièvre to Catherine de Medici, 6 February 1581.
45. *Ibid.,* fol. 285ᵛ, Bellièvre to Henry III, 30 May 1581.
46. *Ibid.,* fols. 103–4, Bellièvre to Catherine de Medici, 31 December 1580.
47. *Ibid.,* fols. 186, 216, Bellièvre to Catherine de Medici, 27 March 1581; Bellièvre to Henry III, 26 April 1581.
48. B.N., Ms. fr. 15906, fol. 493, Henry III to the Prince of Parma, September 1581.

the Protestant assemblies. Like the intendants of a later date, he made a circuit of the provinces, preaching toleration to the Catholics and obedience to the Protestants. Once again, as during his negotiations with Condé and Casimir, Bellièvre had reason to complain, "I have not the means to constrain them." [49] In March 1581, the representatives of the Estates of Languedoc refused Bellièvre's request that they restore the King's cities held as *villes de sûreté*. Those of Dauphiné persisted in their disregard of the treaty of Fleix and found a protector in Henry of Navarre.[50] From the Protestant assembly held at Montauban in May 1581, Bellièvre gained but one small concession—an agreement to hand over the city of Mende.[51] His order to re-establish Catholicism in Montauban was ignored, and three years later the Bishop of Montauban still feared to return to his seat.[52]

Bellièvre's impotence in face of the potentates and regional institutions of the south was but a measure of the crown's incapacity to settle the civil wars. The royal councillor was the loyal representative of a government which could not enforce its writ either in Paris or the provinces. Without the assistance of Anjou and Navarre, he had written Catherine, there was no hope for peace.[53] Unfortunately, the Queen Mother did not command the loyalties of either her son or her son-in-law. In February 1582, Navarre did accept 50,000 *écus* and the return of his properties as the price for the restoration of certain fortified places. Anjou was temporarily appeased by an offer of 100,000 *écus* brought to him by Bellièvre in May.[54] These were the meager results of eighteen months of sustained diplomacy and bargaining.

In the years that followed, Bellièvre bore the principal burden of reconciling Henry of Navarre with the court. Catherine sent the councillor to Guienne in November 1583 for the purpose of mediating between Navarre and his estranged wife, Marguerite of Valois.[55] This scandal in the royal family involved Bellièvre once again in the struggle between the

49. B.N., Ms. fr. 15891, fol. 257, Bellièvre to Henry III, 24 May 1581.
50. *Ibid.*, fol. 161, Bellièvre to Henry III, 9 March 1581.
51. *Ibid.*, fol. 256.
52. *Ibid.*, fol. 375, Bellièvre to the Bishop of Montauban, 1 September 1584.
53. *Ibid.*, fol. 153, Bellièvre to Catherine de Medici, 6 February 1581.
54. B.N., Ms. fr. 15906, fol. 666.
55. *Lettres Médicis,* VIII, 425–28.

Protestant and royalist factions in the southwest. Navarre insisted that any rapprochement with his wife be contingent upon the evacuation of several towns held by the royalist troops of Marshal Matignon. Fearful lest an incident or accident plunge France more deeply into civil war, Bellièvre worked to assuage Navarre's suspicions concerning Matignon.[56] Finally, in early January 1584, the Huguenot leader consented to meet with Bellièvre, and the royal councillor gained his assent to a reconciliation. Catherine expressed her satisfaction to Bellièvre: "I will commence my letter by telling you that, after God, you have returned me to good health by having, through your prudence and good conduct, brought an end to so good a work and so important for all our house and our honor."[57]

From the marital affairs of the King of Navarre, Bellièvre was forced to turn to his former preoccupations with the south and the *villes de sûreté*. In August 1584 he went before a Protestant assembly at Montauban to secure, four years after the fact, assent to the provisions of the Peace of Fleix. To the Huguenot deputies and their leader, Navarre, he recalled "the saying of an old philosopher, that he who wishes to become just must first confess himself unjust." Their disobedience, brigandage, and violence, Bellièvre protested, served only the cause of France's enemies. Therefore, he concluded, "Cease these evils and attain the good which must be desired by all true and natural Frenchmen."[58] His appeal to aristocratic loyalty and national unity was completely ineffective. By the summer of 1584, the complexion of the civil war had changed, and the stakes of victory included the throne itself.

The death in June 1584 of François of Valois, Duke of Anjou and of Brabant, raised the problem of the succession to the throne and thereby extinguished whatever hope of peace and reconciliation the efforts of the Queen Mother and her agents had raised. In death, as in life, Anjou proved to be the most troublesome of Catherine's family, and his demise set in motion the revolutionary activities of the Catholic faction of Guise-Lorraine. In July 1585 Henry III was to capitulate to the Duke of

56. B.N., Ms. fr. 3357, fols. 81, 89, Bellièvre to Matignon, 18, 20 January 1584.
57. *Lettres Médicis*, VIII, 181.
58. B.N., Ms. fr. 15891, fols. 371–73.

Guise and ban the Protestant heresy. But during the months preceding this surrender, Catherine worked to solve the question of succession through the conversion of the King of Navarre to Catholicism. To this end, Bellièvre entered into a round of negotiations with a representative of Navarre, Jean de Clervant.

While the Queen Mother journeyed to Epernay to negotiate a settlement with the Duke of Guise and his party, Bellièvre undertook to persuade the King of Navarre to reconcile himself with Henry III and return to the Catholic faith. The councillor began his peacemaking efforts in April 1585, at a time when the internal conditions in France were near chaos. From Paris, Bellièvre reported to the Queen Mother that her daughter Marguerite had established an autonomous government at Agen; that her son, the King, had abandoned the affairs of state to become a penitent; and that his home city of Lyons had gone over to the Catholic League.[59] It was this crisis of government which formed the background to Bellièvre's negotiations with Clervant. Initially, the emissary from Navarre offered some hope to Bellièvre, who insisted that the Protestant leader abandon the evil counsels of the Huguenots and "enter into the arms of Monseigneur the Cardinal of Bourbon."[60] Both Clervant and his master, however, feared that Catherine intended to appease the Guise faction at the expense of the Protestants. Early in May, Bellièvre warned the Queen Mother that the King of Navarre remained firmly attached to the Protestant cause, and that the Huguenots, favored and protected by foreign powers, had strengthened their position.[61] War with the Huguenots would be difficult to avoid, Bellièvre judged, for it was rumored that Duke Casimir of the Palatine would march into France within two months. By the latter part of May, the negotiations between Clervant and the royal councillor had reached an impasse, and on the twenty-seventh of the month Bellièvre reported to Catherine on his failure.[62] The complete breakdown of negotiations in June and Bellièvre's dire warnings concerning the military threat of the Protestants could only

59. *Ibid.,* fols. 389, 395, 397, Bellièvre to Catherine de Medici, 3, 15, 18 April 1585.
60. *Ibid.,* fol. 399, Bellièvre to Catherine de Medici, 3 May 1585.
61. *Ibid.,* fol. 401, Bellièvre to Catherine de Medici, 5 May 1585.
62. *Ibid.,* fol. 403, Bellièvre to Catherine de Medici, 27 May 1585.

have increased Catherine's resolve to come to an understanding with the Guise party. The result was the humiliating Treaty of Nemours of July 1585 by which the crown acceded to the harshest demands of the Catholic faction.

Despite his failure to gain satisfaction from Clervant and the hardening of his attitude toward the Huguenots, Bellièvre continued his efforts to secure the conversion of the King of Navarre. In a letter to his future master, probably written early in 1586, he wrote "After God, the salvation of this state depends upon a good understanding between the King and you." [63] Navarre's refusal to espouse the Catholic faith, Bellièvre warned, had alienated many of those over whom he might one day rule. Nor would the military support of the Protestant princes of Germany be sufficient to force the French to accept a Calvinist king. Henry's obstinate attitudes on the religious question threatened to subvert the Salic law, which in Bellièvre's mind was the central instrument for the preservation of legitimate and orderly government. [64]

Behind Bellièvre's appeal for reason on the part of the King of Navarre lay the specter of Spanish domination of the French kingdom. From December 1584, when Philip II and the Duke of Guise formalized their relations by the Treaty of Joinville, Spanish intervention in the internal affairs of France had steadily increased. [65] "The more ruin and wrong which the Catholics suffer at the hands of the Germans," Bellièvre wrote to Navarre, "the more you will be detested and hated by the French, and the more they band together and seek to strengthen themselves by the support of the Spaniards." To preserve the integrity of the state, Navarre had to come to terms with Henry III, who had resolved to ban the Protestant faith. Political reason, simple prudence, and the self-interest of the legitimate heir to the throne required that ideological considerations and factional strife be removed from French politics. If personal ambition and religious faith were not subordinated to the good of the state, Bellièvre feared that the total ruin of the kingdom would

---

63. B.N., Ms. fr. 15895, fol. 111, Bellièvre to Henry of Navarre, 1586.
64. *Ibid.,* fol. 115.
65. On the Treaty of Joinville, see De Lamar Jensen, *Diplomacy and Dogmatism: Bernardino de Mendoza and the French Catholic League* (Cambridge, 1964), pp. 54–55.

soon follow.[66] The conventional political wisdom of the *politique,* manifested in the councillor's plea to Navarre, went unheeded. Not until 1589, when Henry III and his cousin allied to combat the Catholic League, did the reconciliation advocated by Bellièvre take place.

At the royal court, Bellièvre worked assiduously to dispel the hostility with which Henry III regarded his Protestant cousin and potential successor. During the course of his negotiations with Jean de Clervant, Bellièvre urged the crown not to impose excessive conditions upon any agreement of reconciliation with Navarre. To Catherine he wrote, "If this affair is treated in anything but general terms, I fear that its success will not be such as we must desire." [67] At every turn, the royal councillor, with counsels of moderation, sought to dissolve the hard lines which separated the two Henrys. In an account of his activities during the crucial months which followed the signing of the Treaty of Nemours, Bellièvre related that he had approached the King at Chenonceaux and had urged him to recall Navarre to court and to treat him "according to the rank and place which he held in the kingdom." Henry III then demanded to know whether Navarre was prepared to accept the Catholic faith. "I said to him," wrote Bellièvre, "that this was something he had not yet declared to me, but that it seemed necessary that His Majesty approach him . . . otherwise I had no hope in this affair." [68]

Bellièvre's confidence that bitter civil strife and the rivalries of the kingdom's great families could be resolved through protocol and platitudes was of course misplaced. The ambitions of the Guises and the recalcitrance of Henry of Navarre frustrated the efforts of the Queen Mother and her chief advisers to unite the kingdom under one king and one religion. Nevertheless, Catherine strove tirelessly for an accommodation. "Certainly it is no time for our hearts to fail," she wrote to Bellièvre in March 1587. "I know that you have more courage than your robe usually demonstrates, just as, God be thanked, God has given me more than is usual in my sex for affairs which are considered dangerous." [69]

During his final, turbulent months as councillor of Henry III, Bellièvre

66. B.N., Ms. fr. 15895, fols. 114–17.
67. B.N., Ms. fr. 15891, fol. 403, Bellièvre to Catherine de Medici, 27 May 1585.
68. B.N., Ms. fr. 15893, fols. 144, 144ᵛ.
69. *Lettres Médicis,* IX, 196.

undertook numerous missions, both in France and abroad, to preserve the peace and the throne of the last Valois. In November 1586 the King dispatched his councillor to England to plead with Queen Elizabeth for the life of Mary Stuart.[70] To Stafford, Bellièvre's mission appeared to offer some hope for an Anglo-French entente. "I think this man's coming over will bring more effect than anybody else that could be sent," he informed Lord Burghley, "as he is a great enemy to the Spaniards and to Spain, and I think will be very willing to divert the civil war of this realm to something against Spain."[71] Bernardino de Mendoza, the Spanish ambassador to France and paymaster of the League, was equally convinced that Bellièvre's journey had a secret purpose. Some months earlier, he had written Philip II, "There is indeed no person of judgment who doubts that the King is plotting something with Secretary Villeroy, and that Bellièvre is in league with them." Thus, it appeared probable to the Spanish King that the instructions given Bellièvre by the French crown went beyond the question of the fate of the Scottish Queen.[72]

During the period which encompassed his mission to England, Bellièvre was employed by the crown to strengthen the ties between England and France. There is, however, no evidence to suggest that the royal councillor advanced the cause of Anglo-French friendship during the course of his mission on behalf of Mary Stuart. Whatever his secret instructions, Bellièvre achieved little in England, and his diplomatic efforts only served to embitter the relations between the two countries. On three occasions he was received at the English court, where he delivered a lengthy address in a vain attempt to stay the execution of the Scottish Queen.[73] Toward the middle of January 1587, Bellièvre and the French ambassador to England, Guillaume L'Aubespine, had a private and fruitless meeting with Elizabeth. Then, amidst rumors of a French plot to

---

70. The principal documents concerning this mission are to be found in *Relations politiques de la France et de l'Espagne avec l'Ecosse au XVIᵉ siècle,* ed. Alexandre Teulet (Paris, 1862), IV, 61–169. (Hereafter cited as *Relations avec l'Ecosse.*)

71. *C.S.P., For.,* XXI, 147.

72. *Calendar of Letters and State Papers Relating to English Affairs,* ed. Martin S. Hume (London, 1896, 1899), III, 147; IV, 11.

73. Bellièvre's speech on this occasion is to be found in *Relations avec l'Ecosse,* IV, 115–28.

assassinate the English sovereign, Bellièvre returned to France to report his failure to the King.[74]

By the early months of 1587, the activities of the League threatened France with a cataclysmic civil war. "Since my return from England," Bellièvre wrote the Duke of Nevers in February, "I have not found the affairs of this kingdom better disposed to peace and patience than they were when I left. . . . Once foreign forces are assembled on both sides, it will be impossible to arrive at any peace which is not more prejudicial than war."[75] To meet the crisis, the Queen Mother once again entered into negotiations with the militant League. In May, Catherine, accompanied by Bellièvre, set off for Rheims to seek a settlement of the issues which divided the leaguers and the royalists. Together with Catherine, the royal councillor carried much of the burden of negotiating with the Duke of Guise, the Cardinal of Guise, the Cardinal of Bourbon, and other leaders of the Catholic faction.[76] Although the Queen Mother and her agents did succeed in prolonging a truce between the League and the Duke of Bouillon, the leader of the Protestant forces in the northwest, the Guises were obdurate on other matters, such as the restitution of the towns and cities which they occupied.[77] At Rheims, Catherine's diplomacy suffered another serious reversal. Deeply involved with Spain in a conspiracy against the state, the Guises remained defiant and rejected the Queen Mother's conciliatory overture.

In the months prior to the Day of the Barricades, May 12, 1588, the French court was the scene of intense political and diplomatic activity designed, on the one hand, to reduce the Protestant rebellion and, on the other, to withdraw the Guise faction from its entanglement with Spain. Bellièvre, who had long served as middleman between the crown and Henry of Navarre, now engaged in a series of negotiations with the Guises and their allies. Henry III sent his councillor to the Duke of Mayenne in November 1587 to offer him financial support for his campaign against the German mercenaries, allies of the King of Navarre.

74. *Ibid.*, pp. 144–45, 146–53; *C.S.P., For.*, XXI, 184–85, 189.
75. B.N., Ms. fr. 3398, fol. 63, Bellièvre to Nevers, 14 February 1587.
76. B.N., Ms. fr. 15892, fol. 121, Bellièvre to Villeroy, 27 May 1587.
77. *Lettres Médicis*, IX, 206–7.

Bellièvre was also instructed to dissaude Mayenne from sending troops into France to join the royal army, at that time engaged in the struggle against the Huguenots.[78] In February 1588 Bellièvre and Philbert de la Guiche were dispatched to the headquarters of the League in an attempt to strengthen the frontiers against the German princes and to secure the obedience which the dissident cousins of the King, Guise and Mayenne, owed to the crown.[79] Throughout March and April, Bellièvre persisted in his efforts to resolve the differences between the monarchy and the most dangerous of the overmighty subjects. Although the principal issue at stake was the conspiratorial activity of the League, negotiations centered upon the rebellious activities of the Duke of Aumale in Picardy. The Duke of Guise responded evasively to Bellièvre's plea that he restrain his cousin Aumale, who in defiance of Henry III had occupied several towns in the northern province. At the end of April, the royal councillor wrote to Catherine, "I have done what I could . . . to compose the affairs of Picardy. . . . I fear that my success is not what we might desire for the contentment of the King and the repose of the kingdom." [80] Thereupon, Bellièvre asked to be recalled from his mission.

Bellièvre's several missions to the Duke of Guise were simply exercises in futility, and their failure represented the final bankruptcy of Catherine's politics of appeasement. By the spring of 1588, as De Lamar Jensen has shown, Guise was under the direct orders of the Spanish King, and his most drastic act, the entry into Paris in May, was but part of Philip II's grand design which would culminate in the sending of the Armada against England.[81] Before the Day of the Barricades, Bellièvre, at the King's command, made the short journey to Soissons to prevent the Duke from entering Paris. On May 9 Stafford reported to Elizabeth, "Bellièvre returned on Saturday, marvellous evil contented with the Duke of Guise's manner of dealing with him, and did plainly tell the King . . . that either he must give them what was not fit for a King to grant . . . or else to

78. B.N., Ms. fr. 3975, fol. 174.

79. Monnier, *Missions,* pp. 127–28; "Projet de l'instruction de Monsieur de Bellièvre allant vers Monsieur de Guise," B.N., Ms. fr. 15892, fols. 145–46.

80. *Lettres Médicis,* IX, 335.

81. Jensen, *Diplomacy and Dogmatism,* p. 137.

show himself a King." Upon hearing Bellièvre's remarks, Stafford continued, Henry III "grew into a great choler and told his mother that they might see what her delays and expectations came unto. That he would take another course." [82] The Queen Mother, however, prevailed upon her son to send Bellièvre once again to the Duke of Guise.

Catherine's final gesture of conciliation was in vain. On May 9 the Duke entered Paris and confronted the King at the Louvre. That very day the English ambassador met Bellièvre at the royal palace and conveyed the following report to Walsingham: "Bellièvre, booted, coming in to the King from the Queen Mother, I asked him if he was so soon come home. He shook 'the head' very soberly and told me that he that he went to was come unlooked for, and so went by in haste to the King." [83]

The entry of Guise into Paris and the ensuing humiliations which Henry III endured at the hands of the League brought the French monarchy to its nadir and, in time, led the erratic and unstable King to repudiate the policies of the past—policies which had been closely identified with Catherine. One result of Henry III's new militancy was the banishment of those councillors and secretaries who had been the principal instruments of the Queen Mother's political designs. Thus, on September 9, some weeks before the fateful meeting of the Estates General at Blois, the first phase of Bellièvre's career as crown servant came to an end.

V

A RUMOR "that a great sudden change was at the Court" reached the English ambassador in Paris on September 1. [84] Within a week, Henry III curtly dismissed his major advisers and administrators, including the chancellor, Cheverny; the secretaries of state, Villeroy, Pierre Brulart, and Pinart; and his councillor, Bellièvre. [85] The King's action came unexpectedly, for Bellièvre, only days before his forced retirement, had written to a

82. *C.S.P., For.*, XXI, 604, 605.
83. *Ibid.*, p. 606.
84. *Ibid.*, XXII, 178.
85. For recent discussions of Henry's move, see Jensen, *Diplomacy and Dogmatism*, pp. 161–62, and Sutherland, *Secretaries of State*, pp. 284–303.

crown lawyer that he planned to attend the meeting of the Estates General and had drafted a project for the reformation of the ordinances of the kingdom.[86] Many explanations for the banishment of the most experienced of the high state officials circulated at Blois. The most preposterous of these was Henry III's assertion that Bellièvre was a Huguenot. Later in September, Lord Burghley recorded the following notes on the charges leveled by the French King against his leading advisers: [87]

> The Chancellor—"Charged thus by the French King: racked all the world for his own profit."
>
> Villeroy—"Presumptuous to rule all."
>
> Brulart—"For ten crowns would betray all."
>
> Pinart—"Ignorant."
>
> Bellièvre—"Thought to be a Huguenot."

More to the point were the observations of Bellièvre's nephew, Jacques Faye, who reported from Blois that the King had found humiliating the edict of reunion concluded in July 1588 between the crown and the Duke of Guise and consequently had removed those of his servants who had encouraged or participated in the negotiations. It was also a source of concern at court, Faye wrote his uncle, that those who had so frequently traveled to Chalons and Soissons to confer with Guise had failed to detect his determination to confront Henry III in Paris.[88]

Any attempt to assign completely rational motives to an action by this least rational of kings is, of course, misplaced. A strong argument can be made, however, that the factors involved in Bellièvre's fall from grace reflected the waning of the aged Catherine's influence over her son and Henry's determination to set out on a new course. In his memoirs, Chancellor Cheverny noted that the principal cause of the great change at court was the King's discontent with his mother's policies, which Henry contended "had overly favored those of the League." As a consequence, the King found suspect those of his council whom the Queen Mother had

---

86. B.N., Ms. fr. 15892, fol. 173, Bellièvre to Marion, 29 August 1588.

87. *C.S.P., For.*, XXII, 208.

88. *Lettres inédites de Jacques et de Charles Faye*, ed. E. Halphen (Paris, 1880), pp. 62–63.

protected and had used to oversee the political affairs of the kingdom.[89]

Bellièvre professed complete ignorance of the causes of the palace revolution. To François Mandelot he wrote, "It would be impossible for me to inform . . . you about the circumstances of this resolution, because I assure you that I do not know." [90] In a letter to the Duke of Nevers, Bellièvre stated that he retired from Blois "with the same good will which I have always had, to remain all my life a very humble and very obedient subject and servant." However, he did mention rumors circulated by his enemies at court and expressed his desire to justify himself before the King.[91] But what in his career had to be justified? Certainly the idea that the councillor was a Huguenot could have entered Henry III's mind only in his maddest moments. Cheverny's explanation of the *coup* makes a good deal more sense. During his negotiations with the League in 1587, Bellièvre had recognized clearly that the Guises were resolved to "commit folly" and to serve the designs of Philip II.[92] Yet he continued to insist, as he wrote to Pinart in the summer of 1588, that "peace would be better than a victory." [93] Bellièvre was bound to, and in the eyes of the King tarnished by, Catherine's prudent politics.

As events in France entered into a dizzy spiral, neither the tired policies of the Queen Mother nor the conciliatory habits of her chief servants were sufficient to the times. The ultimate failure of Catherine, symbolized by the dismissal of Bellièvre, Villeroy, and the others, should not, however, obscure the genuine achievement of Medicean politics. During the long years of civil strife, no clear or easy political choices were open to the French crown. If treachery served Catherine as a weapon of last resort, ceaseless bargaining and cajoling were more her political style. Together with her principal officials, such as Bellièvre, the Queen Mother had maintained an intensive and occasionally successful diplomatic offensive to preserve the rights of her sons and to restore order in the kingdom. If, in the end, diplomacy gave way to assassination and war, the responsibil-

89. Philippe Hurault, "Mémoires de Messire Philippe Hurault, Comte de Cheverny," *Collection complète des mémoires relatifs à l'histoire de France*, ed. M. Petitot (Paris, 1823), XXXVI, 117–18.

90. B.N., Ms. fr. 15892, fol. 179, Bellièvre to Mandelot, 13 September 1588.

91. B.N., Ms. fr. 3336, fol. 103, Bellièvre to Nevers, September 1588.

92. B.N., Ms. fr. 15892, fol. 116, Bellièvre to Villeroy [?], May 1587.

93. *Ibid.*, fol. 419, Bellièvre to Pinart, June 1588.

ity lay with others, not with Catherine. In these years of crisis, her entourage had remained the single school for statesmen in the kingdom.

The banishment of the most influential councillors and secretaries of Henry III prefigured the more violent course which the wars of religion would take. In 1584 Stafford had written of Bellièvre and Villeroy, "These two the King reposes on more than all France, specially in matters of state, and from them nothing is hidden." [94] The crown could ill afford to lose the services of such knowledgeable statesmen, administrators, and politicians. When the events touched off by Guise's defiance of Henry III had run their bloody course, the new king, Henry IV, would again turn to Bellièvre and Villeroy to aid him in the reconstruction of the kingdom. In this manner a degree of continuity between the reigns of the last Valois and the first of the Bourbons was assured.

94. *C.S.P., For.,* **XIX,** 308.

CHAPTER THREE

The Years at Grignon:
1588–1593

FOLLOWING HIS DISMISSAL by Henry III, Bellièvre retired to his estate at Grignon, located in the Ile-de-France some fifteen kilometers from Versailles. This period of exile from the royal court coincided with the passing of the old order of political leadership and the coming to power of the century's greatest king, Henry IV. Within a year of the palace coup of September 1588, the Duke of Guise and Henry III had come to violent ends, and Bellièvre's patroness, Catherine de Medici, was dead. Cut off from the center of power and patronage, the former royal councillor was forced to establish a new connection with the court and courtiers of Henry IV. In time, Grignon became a common meeting place for the political moderates in the realm, as Bellièvre sought to rally his countrymen around the Bourbon monarch; gradually he reinserted himself into the political life of the state. The succession crisis which followed the assassination of Henry III offered Bellièvre the occasion to propound at great length the principles of the *politiques,* and it was as a propagandist of the royalist cause that he entered into the service of his new master.

Over three years passed, however, before Bellièvre resumed an active role in the political affairs of the kingdom. Shortly after the death of Catherine de Medici, he wrote, "I shall leave the discussion of affairs to those who have charge of them since the death of the Queen, our good mistress." [1] For an individual of Bellièvre's cautious temperament, the months after the Queen Mother's death were, indeed, a proper time for political quiescence. There is no evidence to suggest that he ever contemplated joining the League, although other servants of the crown, notably Villeroy, did so. On the other hand, the strength of his personal commitment to Henry IV, at least before 1590, remains in doubt. It would perhaps be best to place Bellièvre among those post-Ivry loyalists whose watchful waiting ended with Henry's first great military triumph over the League.

During the years 1589 and 1590, Bellièvre lived nobly on his estate, the *chatellenie* of Grignon, using what influence he had to preserve his property and tenants from the ravages of civil war. [2] Deprived of the emoluments of office and separated by war from his lands in Lyonnais and Dauphiné, Bellièvre witnessed at first hand the distress of the kingdom and experienced the misery of the officer without office. In return for his thirty-five years of public service, he protested at one point, those in power should at least attempt to preserve his estate from ruin. [3] Nonetheless, his lands were subject to the devastation of war, and troops were quartered there. In July 1589, the royalist commander, Henry of Orléans, wrote Bellièvre, "Tomorrow we shall be your guests. . . . You should advise your subjects to withdraw to your estate. . . . Do not be angry with me for this, for I have not been able to exempt my own lands." [4] The misery of his tenants also weighed upon Bellièvre. "I would rather be a peasant," he wrote to Villeroy's son in 1592, "than live among

1. B.N., Ms. fr. 15892, fol. 316, Bellièvre to [?], January 1589.
2. Grignon had been designated a *chatellenie* by royal letters patent issued in March 1585. For an account of Bellièvre's retirement, with a different emphasis from the present chapter, see J. Nouaillac, "La Retraite de Pomponne de Bellièvre," *Revue historique*, CXVII (1914), 129–67.
3. B.N., Ms. fr. 15892, fol. 241, Bellièvre to Jacques Faye, 12 August 1590.
4. B.N., Ms. fr. 15909, fol. 265.

peasants, suffering in my heart at the evil which is done and participating in their miseries. . . . The poor people gain nothing from the earth; what they sow others reap." [5] The threat to his land and his fortune which the civil war represented, as well as the anguish which he witnessed about him, could only have reinforced Bellièvre's customary pacifism and his respect for the order which legitimacy symbolized.

The question of legitimacy was the dominant political problem of the period of Bellièvre's retirement from the court. It was, of course, raised in July 1589, when Henry III was assassinated and the long-anticipated succession of a Protestant to the throne became at last a reality. Although Bellièvre remained outside the court until early in 1593, he was soon caught up in the politics of the last phase of the religious wars. A shift in masters necessitated no fundamental change in the political philosophy of the former royal councillor, and by 1592 he had become a leading spokesman for royalist sentiment in France.

Unlike Villeroy, who upon dismissal from the court tied his fortunes to those of the Duke of Mayenne and the League, Bellièvre was well suited to resume the role of honest broker among the contending factions. Although cut off from power, he retained his connections with all parties in the state. Thus, at the time of his forced retirement, Bellièvre received sympathetic letters protesting the King's action from such diverse figures as Pierre d'Epinac, the Archbishop of Lyons and a leaguer; the Cardinal of Bourbon, Henry IV's rival for the throne; and Diane of France, sister of the King and related by marriage to the family of Montmorency.[6] From Paris, Jacques Faye informed his uncle that the new royal administrators, Louis Revol and Martin Ruzé, were favorably disposed toward the retired councillor.[7] Above all, Bellièvre had earned, in the course of long and difficult negotiations, the esteem and confidence of Henry IV.[8] As a royalist and elder statesmen with two intimate friends, Villeroy and Epinac, in the camp of the Duke of Mayenne, Bellièvre was in

---

5. Quoted in Nouaillac, "La Retraite," p. 149.

6. B.N., Ms. fr. 15909, fols. 140, 182, 192, 204.

7. *Lettres inédites de Jacques et de Charles Faye*, ed. E. Halphen (Paris, 1880), p. 56. (Hereafter cited as *Lettres Faye.*)

8. *Recueil des lettres missives de Henri IV*, ed. Berger de Xivrey (Paris, 1843), II, 272. (Hereafter cited as *Lettres missives.*)

an excellent position to contribute to a settlement of the succession crisis.

During most of that crisis, Bellièvre openly supported Henry IV's claim to the throne. In 1590 he wrote to Gourdan, "One cannot doubt to whom the crown of France belongs." [9] However, his customary prudence, his health, and his personal situation precluded any active commitment to the royalist cause in the first years of Henry's reign. It was Bellièvre's hope that wise counsels would prevail and avert further bloodshed, but he was forced to recognize that "without the sword the best counsel in the world is liable to fail." A wise and able councillor in times of peace, Bellièvre had little taste for the politics of war. To the royalists he offered his pen and the influence he had with the League—poor weapons indeed when civil war still raged in France. Bellièvre's primary service to Henry IV during the first years of his rule was to help rally the moderates around the royal standard and to open the way for the reconciliation which would come when Henry had established his right to the crown on the battlefield.

The principal figure to whom Bellièvre turned in his attempt to reconcile French Catholics to the Protestant King was Villeroy, who represented the moderate faction within the Duke of Mayenne's party.[10] Although the former secretary of state, rejecting the possibility of a Protestant on the throne, had deserted the crown, he continued to press for the King's conversion and served as the chief negotiator of the League. Villeroy was far more actively engaged in the politics of the early 1590's than was Bellièvre. Both men, however, shared the same fundamental goal—to unify France under a Catholic Henry IV. While Bellièvre refused to follow Villeroy into Mayenne's camp, he insisted that only the King's conversion could preserve the country from total ruin. "As for the desire of an infinite number of subjects in our kingdom that it be the good pleasure of the King to content them on the question of religion," he wrote Villeroy, "you have known my opinion on this since the time of the late King." [11]

9. B.N., Ms. fr. 15892, fol. 423, Bellièvre to Gourdan, 1590.

10. On this phase of Villeroy's career, see J. Nouaillac, *Villeroy, secrétaire d'état et ministre de Charles IX, Henri III et Henri IV* (Paris, 1909), pp. 159–264.

11. B.N., Fonds Dupuy 88, fol. 177, Bellièvre to Villeroy, 30 December 1592.

As early as August 1590, it appeared possible that the two former colleagues would confront one another in negotiations designed to end the civil strife. Villeroy was reported ready to negotiate with the royalists if Bellièvre, Biron, or Cheverny was chosen to represent Henry IV.[12] Mayenne's emissary stipulated that he could not undertake discussions with the Huguenot leader and royal adviser, Philippe du Plessis-Mornay.[13] Jacques Faye informed his uncle that the King had been willing to accept Villeroy's conditions and had designated Bellièvre to be his representative. Rumor had it, however, that du Plessis-Mornay, who desired to be the arbiter of peace, had intervened to frustrate Villeroy's initiative.[14] Whatever the validity of Faye's report, there is no evidence that Bellièvre wished to serve as interlocutor between Henry IV and Mayenne. He complained to Faye that Villeroy's antagonism toward du Plessis-Mornay was a grave disservice to the cause of peace and to the King.[15] Ever cautious and timorous, Bellièvre apparently feared to participate directly in an affair which might have compromised his good standing among the Protestant councillors of Henry IV. This apprehensiveness was reinforced later in the year, when Bellièvre had important family affairs pending at the royal court.

Beginning in 1592, however, Bellièvre played a more active role in the affairs of the kingdom and, through his polemical writings and discourses, served the cause of the royalists and the Protestant King.

II

THREE MAJOR PIECES of Bellièvre's public discourses written during the years 1592 and 1593 have survived. The first of these, which circulated about Paris in December 1592,[16] was a response to Pierre Jeannin, Mayenne's councillor and a future servant of Henry IV. Several months earlier, Jeannin had written Bellièvre a lengthy letter setting forth the

---

12. B.N., Ms. fr. 15892, fol. 291, Bellièvre to Jacques Faye, 12 August 1590; *Lettres Faye,* pp. 107–9.
13. B.N., Ms. fr. 15892, fol. 291.
14. *Lettres Faye,* p. 108.
15. B.N., Ms. fr. 15892, fol. 291.
16. B.N., Ms. fr. 15893, fols. 48–62.

case of Mayenne's faction against Henry IV.[17] In reply to Bellièvre's plea that he use his influence within the League to end the war, Jeannin had contended that if Catholics were to recognize Henry IV as King, the very existence of the faith would be endangered and the authority of the papacy undermined. "Catholics must never reject in this matter which concerns religion," he had written, "the counsels and authority of the Holy Father." All attempts at reconciliation would be in vain unless the King appeased the papacy and converted. Those who had joined ranks with Mayenne were, in Jeannin's opinion, men of good will who loved the state and the Catholic religion, and who desired, above all, the repose of the kingdom. The Duke of Mayenne supposedly shared these ideals. Although Jeannin recognized that "We stand at the edge of a torrent," he placed the burden of restoring peace in France squarely upon Henry of Navarre. "Believe me, Monsieur," he had written to Bellièvre, "the beginning and end of this good work is the conversion of the King of Navarre."

In his letter to Bellièvre, Jeannin reflected the despair of the moderates in the League who recognized that they were at the abyss, but who, because of principle or loyalty to Mayenne, felt powerless to influence events. It was to such moderates, who in the end stood upon their historic faith, that Bellièvre directed his appeal for reason—that reason which would assure the survival not only of the state but of the Catholic faith as well.

To Jeannin's primary argument—that Henry IV should convert—Bellièvre readily agreed. He wrote, "It is necessary that the King conform to the desire of his Catholic subjects who constitute four-fifths or more of his kingdom . . . for without this resolution of His Majesty we can expect only ruin and division in this kingdom." The former councillor claimed that he had made an attempt to see Henry IV in order to discuss the religious question, but that the King, engaged in the siege of Paris, had been too preoccupied to consider conversion. However, Bellièvre expressed his hope that, like Constantine and Clovis, Henry would convert and that the Catholic faith would be re-established throughout the kingdom.

17. B.N., Ms. fr. 15895, fols. 195–204, Jeannin to Bellièvre, 25 September 1592.

The fundamental question which divided moderate Catholics, such as Bellièvre, and the supporters of the League was not the desirability of the King's conversion but rather the right of a faction, for religious reasons, to oppose the legitimate succession to the throne. Bellièvre conceded that many men of good will had joined the League, but he denied the validity of their position. Furthermore, he cast doubt upon the sincerity of the Duke of Mayenne's alleged desire for peace. Whereas Jeannin had written of those princes "who serve us," Bellièvre argued that it was the League which served foreign princes. Behind the ideological stance of the leaguers, he detected the machinations of foreign powers bent on the destruction of the French monarchy. If the leaguers persisted in listening to the advice of foreigners, he warned Jeannin, they would bear the responsibility for a perpetual civil war in France.

Having transferred the burden of responsibility from Henry IV to Mayenne and his party, Bellièvre went on to consider the problem of the Roman Church in the French state. The civil war, he contended, had been the cause of tremendous economic dislocation and of an appalling moral laxity. Churchmen were deprived of their financial resources; corruption, atheism, and lawlessness were rampant. By way of contrast to the general condition of the Church in France, Bellièvre noted that in those cities obedient to the crown, "We see the Catholic religion re-established, ecclesiastics enjoying their churches and revenues, and the rest of the Catholics . . . consoled by the restoration of their Catholic religion." Was it not more expedient, he asked Jeannin, to negotiate a peace with Henry IV than to allow the Catholic faith to perish in the anarchy of civil war? In this manner, Bellièvre introduced the pragmatic arguments of the *politiques.* Ideological extremism threatened the very survival of the Church in France and served only the interests of the Spanish monarchy. Moreover, the welfare of all Christendom was involved in the struggle between the factions. On the eastern borders of Europe the Turks stood ready to draw whatever advantages they could from the fratricidal warfare among Christians. Thus, for the good of the Catholic religion, for the conservation of the kingdom, and for their own "repose, contentment, and greatness," Mayenne and his followers had to come to terms with Henry IV.[18]

18. B.N., Ms. fr. 15893, fols. 48, 49, 50, 54, 55, 56, 57, 61.

Bellièvre's appeal to Jeannin had been prompted by the Duke of Mayenne's summoning, in November 1592, an Estates General to elect a new king.[19] This act represented not only a grave challenge to the principle of legitimacy but also a high point of Spanish and papal intervention in French political affairs. In his semipublic letter to Jeannin, Bellièvre warned that the Pope, by supporting the election of a new king, would doom France to ruin. At the same time, December 1592, he appealed to his old friend Villeroy in the hope of arousing the moderates within the League against the forthcoming Estates General.[20] Offering the hope that Henry IV could give assurances to Mayenne on the religious question, Bellièvre stressed the dangers of foreign intervention in the civil war. "As for what you write concerning the coming of a foreign army," he wrote Villeroy, "please understand my misgivings. . . . When you assemble your forces, the King will gather his together and this will bring to an end any talk about peace."[21]

The extreme actions of the Duke of Mayenne and the blatant intrusion of the papacy and Spain in the succession crisis stimulated what Henri Drouot has termed a "Gallican reaction"[22]—a reaction which raised in a most dramatic way ancient questions of church and state. The prospect of an even more disastrous war and the revolutionary implications of Mayenne's convocation of the Estates General led Bellièvre to produce the most detailed exposition of the theoretical assumptions which lay behind his essentially pragmatic approach to the political and religious problems of his age. His "Un Escrit contre la convocation des prétendus estats de la ligue"[23] was one important manifestation of the Gallican reaction against the political pretensions of the papacy.

Bellièvre opened his discourse in defense of the rights of Henry IV by quoting Saint Jerome's dictum that "One of the principal signs of a true Catholic is that he obey his prince faithfully." He then developed his argument in the following manner:

19. Henri Drouot, *Mayenne et la bourgogne: étude sur la ligue* (Paris, 1937), II, 197–223.
20. B.N., Fonds Dupuy 88, fols. 177–83, Bellièvre to Villeroy, 30 December 1592.
21. *Ibid.*, fol. 179.
22. Drouot, *Mayenne*, II, 213–20.
23. B.N., Ms. fr. 15893, fols. 68–96 (1592).

> We hold that Catholics who have not departed from obedience to their
> King, who remain firm in their religion, who beg . . . His Majesty to
> become reconciled to the Holy Apostolic See, should be judged better
> Catholics, and more devoted to the preservation of the religion of our
> fathers, than those who have banded together to make war on their
> King.

Moreover, Bellièvre insisted that "The kingdom of France is not elective.
It is God and not the French people who has given and gives this Crown
to our Kings." Thus he countered the propositions of the Catholic rebels
by appealing to the ancient religious sanctions against civil disobedience
and to what was essentially a theory of the divine right of kings. In
addition, Bellièvre introduced into his argument against the League the
concept of the fundamental law, a key tenet of which provided that the
succession should pass to the nearest male relative of the deceased monarch.[24] It was impossible, he claimed, to elect a king when, under the Salic
law, only a prince of the blood could succeed to the throne.

According to Bellièvre's analysis of the dictates of the Church Fathers
and the unwritten constitution, the right of subjects to revolt against
legitimately constituted authority and to elect a king was clearly prohib-
ited. Yet an election had been proposed, and it was rumored that the
enemies of the crown sought from Rome the excommunication of all
Catholic advisers and supporters of Henry IV. Bellièvre recalled the
historical parallel between this situation and the fourteenth-century struggle of Boniface VIII and Philip the Fair. A pope, he declared, could not
command disobedience to a king. Of Pope Clement VIII, Bellièvre wrote,
"We wish to defer to him according to the great power which it has
pleased God to bestow upon him. . . . But the dignity of the Holy Father
does not diminish that of kings." On the subject of excommunication, he
insisted that the individual Catholic could disobey unjust papal injunctions. God was the ultimate judge, and He would not condemn men of
good will who resisted the misguided decrees of the Pope. "If it should
happen that the Pope commands something which is contrary to the Holy
Scriptures," Bellièvre stated, "we must not obey him. Following what is
written in the Acts of the Apostles, one must obey God rather than men."

24. On the notion of the fundamental law, see Ralph Giesey, "The Juristic
Basis of Dynastic Right to the French Throne," *Transactions of the American
Philosophical Society*, LI, Pt. 5 (1961), 25–38.

He equated obedience to the crown with obedience to God. Consequently, the duty of the good Catholic was to support the monarchy. Upon the three orders of the realm, the former councillor urged a policy of courageous resistance to the decrees of the papacy.

In Bellièvre's mind, those who massacred and pillaged in the name of religion were not only hypocrites but "true atheists." "The Catholic servants of the King," he wrote, "desire a reconciliation with . . . the Duke of Mayenne. . . . They desire the eradication of heresies . . . but they cannot in good conscience use the name of religion to bring confusion and ruin to the state, the conservation of which will also preserve religion." A good Catholic could serve his king and still remain loyal to his faith.

In any case, the central issue in Mayenne's rebellion was not religion but sedition, sponsored and encouraged by France's greatest enemy, the Spanish monarchy. "We hold the Catholics who have remained firm in their religion and in the service of the King to be much better Catholics," Bellièvre wrote, "than if, to beg a pension from the Spaniard, they resolved to make a war which would be of sedition, rather than religion." The end result of the excommunication of Henry IV and the proposed excommunication of the Catholic loyalists, he argued, would be to transfer the French crown to the King of Spain. If the maxims of the Church Fathers and the French constitution dictated obedience to Henry IV, history and experience did likewise. "History teaches us," Bellièvre concluded, "that he who calls upon the strongest for aid most often becomes the subject of the strongest."

The discourse against the Estates of the League embodied the principles of *gallicanisme politique.* Unoriginal in its content, the discourse was nonetheless important because of the prestige of its author. Bellièvre's emphasis upon the inviolability of the fundamental law and dynastic rights placed him squarely in the tradition of those *légistes* who, from the time of Philip the Fair, had sought to establish a strong legal basis for monarchical power.

It had been Bellièvre's intention in his attack upon the Estates of the League to cast doubt upon the motives of the Catholic rebels and to expound a counterideology in terms at once Christian, legalistic, patriotic, and practical. The fulfillment of his hopes, however, depended upon the

King's conversion. Once Henry of Navarre accepted the Catholic faith, the importance of the religious question diminished, and the Duke of Mayenne and those who remained loyal to him were obviously open to the charge of sedition. Henry's return to the faith, which took place at Saint-Denis in July 1593, won over many of the dissident Catholics, but it did not still all opposition to the monarchy. To those who continued to resist union under the first of the Bourbons, Bellièvre addressed yet another pamphlet, "L'Advis aux François sur la déclaration faicte par le roy en l'église S. Denys en France." [25]

In his "Notice to the French," Bellièvre reiterated the themes which he had developed in his earlier political discourses. His main line of argument was directed against Philip II of Spain, whom he accused of fostering disunion in order to usurp the French throne. The Spanish King, he charged, had taken advantage of the religious wars to intervene in French politics in the guise of the protector of the Christian faith. "All good Frenchmen must bear in mind," Bellièvre admonished, "that it is God first of all, it is birth, it is the law which gives us the King. This power does not rest in the hands of the people, and even less in the hands of a foreign prince, whoever he may be." Again Bellièvre warned of the dangers of civil disobedience. "We must resolve that there is nothing more important for the conservation of the Catholic religion and the state," he wrote, "than the obedience which will be universally rendered to His Majesty by all the subjects of this Crown; without which we can expect only evil, ruin, dissipation, dissolution, and disorder in religion and the state." A united France would serve as a bulwark of the Roman Catholic Church; a divided France would only further the decline of religion.

The "Notice to the French" was the last of Bellièvre's major public discourses of the years 1592 and 1593, and, like the others, it was written to defend the royalist position against specific acts of the Catholic League. Despite their polemical and immediate nature, however, these writings constitute the single best source of Bellièvre's formal political ideas and a good summation of the *politique* position as it was expounded by lawyers and officers loyal to the crown. The events which culminated in the convocation of the Estates of the League and the crisis over the conversion

25. B.N., Ms. fr. 15893, fols. 136, a–r (1593).

of Henry of Navarre forced loyalists such as Bellièvre to formulate in a coherent fashion their views on kingship, sovereignty, the higher law, and the relations of Church and state. The result was a mélange of ideas which harked back to the Gallican tradition and, as Bellièvre rightly noted, to the era of Philip IV. Into this body of royalist and Gallican thought were incorporated certain contemporary notions—principally that of the fundamental law. Indeed, this conception of a higher law represented the cornerstone and unifying theme of Bellièvre's defense of legitimacy. In a letter to the Duke of Nevers, he justified his stand against the League as resistance to those who undermined the laws of the state.[26]

In matters of religion, Bellièvre was a loyal Catholic who feared lest the Pope "reduce us to the necessity of disobeying him, or in obeying him disobey God and our King." [27] To the degree that the papacy sanctioned disobedience to the crown and disregarded the established laws of the state, it was regarded by Bellièvre more as a hostile power than the center of authority within the universal Church. Without attacking the character of the popes or denying their spiritual authority, he contested the validity of papal decrees which were politically inspired. As early as 1591, Bellièvere had composed an epistle to Gregory XIV firmly remonstrating against the papacy's support of the Spanish faction in Rome and of the League's envoys.[28] Another long discourse, undated and probably never published, protested the excommunication of Henry IV as a violation of the Salic law and as a device to serve Spanish ambitions in France.[29] Again, in 1593, Bellièvre defended, against the objections of the papacy, the absolution of the King by the royalist clergy. Henry was unable to journey to Rome to be absolved directly by Clement VIII, Bellièvre wrote Nevers, because of the troubles in the kingdom.[30] For the good of the state and the Roman Church, it had been necessary to proceed with the absolution in France. Wherever papal pretensions and state interest clashed, the *politique* found good cause to subordinate the wishes and injunctions of Rome to political considerations.

26. *Ibid.,* fol. 137, Bellièvre to Nevers, 24 August 1593.
27. *Ibid.,* fol. 95.
28. B.N., Ms. fr. 15892, fols. 491–537.
29. B.N., Ms. fr. 15895, fols. 118–25.
30. B.N., Ms. fr. 15893, fol. 138, Bellièvre to Nevers, 24 August 1593.

Bellièvre not only urged resistance to the papacy in its acts against Henry IV but also advised the crown not to risk future troubles by burdening itself with obligations in the sphere of religion. To the League's demand that Henry IV accept the condition that subjects would henceforth be absolved of their oath of fidelity to a king turned heretic, Bellièvre replied, "I cannot advise the King to agree to this. It seems to me that this would provide an opportunity for those who wish to embarrass France to use this as a pretext and, with the support of a Pope unfavorable to France, overthrow the kingdom." [31] The leaguers had also demanded that the King outlaw the practice of any religion but Roman Catholicism. Bellièvre agreed that the continued existence of the heretical faith posed a threat to the stability of France. "But we must consider the state of the kingdom," he wrote. "Even if the King should order this, it would be no more possible for him to execute it than it was for the late King and his brother. . . . The ordinance would serve only to rekindle war among Frenchmen." Bellièvre suggested that the King express his desire to reunite all of his subjects in the Catholic religion and promise to work closely with the papacy to that end. Ever cautious concerning commitments which might infringe on the sovereign rights of the crown or harden the lines between Catholic and Huguenot, he placed all of his hopes for peace and religious union in the greatest of the *politiques,* Henry IV.

III

DURING THE YEARS in which he served as a spokesman for the royalists, Bellièvre retained his connections with the League. To his fellow royalist, the Cardinal de Gondi, he observed that wisdom was the product of experience and that "The wise man seeks to win the friendship of his enemy." [32] Indeed, a number of the leaguers were not enemies at all; rather, they were friends of long standing with whom Bellièvre maintained mutually respectful relations. Such men as Villeroy or Pierre d'Epinac shared, or pretended to share, Bellièvre's political goals, but they objected to his blurring the religious issue in vague and cautious state-

31. *Ibid.,* fol. 130, Bellièvre to [?], August 1593.
32. *Ibid.,* fol. 64, Bellièvre to Gondi, 1592.

ments. The line between them was best explained by Epinac in the following letter, written in March 1593: [33]

> I agree with you, Monsieur, that we must stop not at what we may desire but at what we may obtain, and that we must not run to extremes. . . . But we must recognize also that there are some things so essential that they cannot be omitted without harm and shame. Among them I number the conservation of the religion. . . . Religion must not be left to chance under doubtful conditions. . . .

The differences between the two friends were clear, but they were not so great as to preclude a continuing dialogue or the possibility of negotiations. Within the moderate wing of the League, Bellièvre found men of like temperament and experience with whom he could join in the search for a negotiated peace.

Bellièvre's active involvement in the political affairs of the country began in April 1592, when he served as host to a group of moderates who met at Montfort, near Grignon, to discuss the possibilities of negotiations to end the civil war. Although he had taken up the royalist cause well before this time, Bellièvre's political role had been negligible. His primary efforts had been devoted to protecting his family's fortune, to cultivating the good will of the crown, and to rebuilding his connections at the court. In October 1590 Bellièvre issued an apology for his conduct in the affair of Marguerite of Navarre, a self-serving act obviously designed to placate any hostility toward him at the royal court.[34] His prudent attempts to secure royal favor, as has been noted, most likely prevented him from actively engaging in the early negotiations involving the royalists and Villeroy. Another factor accounting for his relative inactivity was a serious illness which left the former councillor in poor health and forced him to ponder leaving "this world where I have . . . lived for others and too little for myself." [35] If self-interest, implied in the apology of 1590, and conviction, set forth in the "Epistle to Gregory XIV" of 1591, placed Bellièvre in the royalist camp by the beginning of the decade, it was only in 1592, with the meeting at Montfort, that he reasserted his influence in public life.

33. B.N., Ms. fr. 15910, fol. 22, Epinac to Bellièvre, 20 March 1593.
34. B.N., Ms. fr. 15892, fols. 402–12^{v}.
35. B.N., Ms. fr. 15893, fol. 45.

The central figure at this meeting of the moderates was the Duke of Nevers. Although a royalist, he had extended little support to Henry of Navarre.[36] Nevers, determinedly working for the conversion of the King, was joined at Montfort by the royalists, Gondi and Camus de Pontcarré, and the chief negotiator of the League, Villeroy. Bellièvre participated in these conversations and found Nevers eager to serve the King and Villeroy anxious to further the cause of peace.[37] The results of his personal intervention with his old colleague, however, were inconclusive. The conference agreed upon a decision to send Gondi to Rome where he was to plead the royalist case before Clement VIII. In addition, all agreed that Henry IV should immediately announce his intention to convert to Roman Catholicism.

The efforts of this gathering came to nothing, for the Duke of Mayenne's terms became increasingly exorbitant, and Clement VIII refused to receive Cardinal de Gondi. Equally fruitless was the conference of Suresnes, which met a year later, in April 1593, and represented a more important attempt to reconcile the warring factions.[38] Despite the objections of extremists in its ranks, the Estates of the League elected twelve deputies, led by Pierre d'Epinac, to meet with a royalist delegation at Suresnes. The latter group numbered among its members the Archbishop of Bourges; the secretary of state, Louis Revol; the historian, Jacques de Thou; and Bellièvre. To the Spanish ambassador, at least, Bellièvre's appearance at Suresnes indicated a change of attitude. In a dispatch to Philip II, the ambassador wrote of Bellièvre, "A wise man, who has remained neutral up to now." [39] Certainly Bellièvre's attacks upon the League and Spain, which had been written some months before, belie the Spaniard's use of the word neutral. The conference at Suresnes did,

36. For Bellièvre's brief account of the Montfort meeting, see *ibid.*, fols. 24–24ᵛ.

37. *Ibid.*

38. The best account of the proceedings at Suresnes is to be found in Palma Cayet's "Chronologie novenaire," *Collection complète des mémoires relatifs à l'histoire de France*, ed. M. Petitot (Paris, 1829), XLI, 304–8. (Hereafter cited as Palma Cayet, *Chronologie.*)

39. *Procès-verbaux des états généraux de 1593*, ed. Auguste Bernard (Paris, 1842), p. 703.

however, mark Bellièvre's return to active service on behalf of the crown, not only as advocate but also as royal agent.

At Suresnes, the proceedings were dominated by Pierre d'Epinac, Archbishop of Lyons, and the Archbishop of Bourges, who engaged in a verbal duel at once learned and sterile. Recapitulating the previously held positions of the two sides, the archbishops drew upon classical sources, the Church Fathers, and Holy Scripture to justify or condemn disobedience to the monarchy on religious grounds. Despite this futile jousting, the conference represented a minor triumph for the royalists. The Archbishop of Bourges arrived at Suresnes with the knowledge that Henry IV intended to abjure his Protestant faith. Bourges joyfully reported the King's decision to the representatives of the League on May 17.[40] In his response to the royalists, Epinac, although desirous of a truce, remained intractable, demanding that the question of the King's conversion be submitted to Clement VIII and that heresy be extirpated from the realm.[41] The reluctance of the League's deputies to enter into negotiations with the King's party on the basis of Henry's announced intention to convert brought the meeting at Suresnes to a standstill. Epinac and Mayenne had been prepared for reconciliation, Bellièvre later wrote Nevers, but not without papal approval. It was this stipulation which convinced the royalists to proceed with the absolution of the King by the French bishops alone.[42]

Bellièvre's role in the open meetings at Suresnes was a modest one. Palma Cayet mentioned his participation in the conference but once, and this single reference indicates that Bellièvre subordinated himself to the Archbishop of Bourges, who eloquently presented the royalist arguments.[43] Behind the scenes, however, he engaged in private conversations with Villeroy and others in an effort to hammer out the conditions of a truce.[44] Toward the end of June, the royalist deputies who had been present at Suresnes issued, from Saint-Denis, a pamphlet which, in its

40. Palma Cayet, *Chronologie*, pp. 359–67.
41. B.N., Ms. fr. 15895, fol. 310, Bellièvre to Nevers, 24 August 1593.
42. *Ibid.*, fols. 310, 312–13.
43. Palma Cayet, *Chronologie*, p. 322.
44. On Villeroy's participation, see Nouaillac, *Villeroy*, p. 242.

reasoned exposition of the King's case, was reminiscent of Bellièvre's earlier polemics.[45] There is, however, no evidence relating to the authorship of this document, and one can only note that among the signatures appended to it was that of Bellièvre.

In this statement, the royalist deputies sought to dissuade the representatives of the League from supporting the election of a new king and warned of the impending dissolution of the kingdom and of the Roman Church which a continuation of the civil war would assure. "The memory of those who work loyally to save their country from extreme danger," they wrote, "will remain perpetual and honorable in the centuries to come, and those living will be loved, respected, and honored . . . as true children of God and true Frenchmen." The immediate goal of the royalist deputies was to obtain the League's agreement to a short truce. "The King has announced that he will grant a truce," they declared, "in order that his poor people be relieved of the miseries which they have suffered in the war. Five weeks ago we issued our proposals. . . . We have awaited your response patiently." Not until August, however, did the representatives of the League, deeply divided among themselves, agree to a three months' cessation of the civil conflict.[46]

From June until the declaration of a truce in August, Bellièvre worked diligently to conciliate the leadership of the League and to urge his views upon the Duke of Mayenne. To the Governor of Paris, the Count of Belin, he sent assurances that the conversion of the King was near—so near "that one must consider it a fact." [47] Those who refused to accept an honorable truce and to declare their submission to Henry IV, Bellièvre suggested, were serving the cause of Spain. Through Belin, he sent the following advice to Mayenne:

> Monsieur, I see that you have written me on the part of the Duke of Mayenne, who knows that I am his very humble servant. . . . I am an old man now and have always wished him happiness and prosperity which, I believe, depend on his conducting himself as a virtuous and just prince, devoted to the preservation of this state . . . of which may posterity say he has been the protector and, after God and the King, the principal defender.

45. B.N., Ms. fr. 15893, fols. 123–28ᵛ.
46. Drouot, *Mayenne*, II, p. 268.
47. B.N., Ms. fr. 15893, fol. 129, Bellièvre to Belin, July 1593.

Within weeks of this message to Belin, Bellièvre and the royalists enjoyed a fleeting triumph as Mayenne accepted the King's terms and agreed to a truce. In the Parlement, Charles Faye reported to his uncle, "Everyone praises the concern and diligence you have brought to this matter." [48]

Neither Henry's conversion nor the truce of August 1 restored peace to the kingdom. By the end of the year, hostilities were resumed. In the interval between the August truce and the final stage of the civil war, Bellièvre participated in a series of meetings designed to convert the truce into a genuine peace. The brief relaxation of tensions allowed the moderates on both sides to meet more frequently in order to interpret and extend the vague provisions of the truce. Bellièvre, Villeroy, Jeannin, and the King's secretary, Revol, first met at Andrésy, toward the middle of August 1593, but were unable to conclude any negotiations because of the Duke of Mayenne's recalcitrance.[49] In September, Bellièvre took part in the conference of Milly. Again, Mayenne's insistence that he could treat only with the approval of the Pope and the Spanish King frustrated attempts to conclude a general peace.[50] Yet another gathering of the diplomats representing the court and the League took place at Poissy in November and proved to be equally fruitless.[51]

Through Bellièvre's correspondence of this period with the Duke of Nevers, one can follow the course of his activities and the disintegration of the fragile truce. Toward the end of August he sent to Nevers in Rome a copy of his "Notice to the French" and a lengthy denunciation of the papal legate, Cardinal Plaisance, whom Bellièvre accused of sacrificing France in order to obtain the papal throne for himself.[52] On September 1, Bellièvre wrote that he had recently returned from a conference with the deputies of the League where he had presented his "Notice to the French."[53] Early in November, Bellièvre was at Grignon awaiting the arrival of Belin and the opening of the meetings at Poissy. By this time, he had come to share the growing impatience of the court with the tactics of Mayenne and the intrigues of the Spanish faction in Rome. "The Holy

48. *Lettres Faye*, p. 135.
49. Nouaillac, *Villeroy*, p. 247.
50. *Ibid.*
51. B.N., Ms. fr. 3987, fol. 21, Bellièvre to Nevers, 6 November 1593.
52. B.N., Ms. fr. 15893, fols. 137–142, Bellièvre to Nevers, August 1593.
53. B.N., Ms. fr. 3985, fol. 200, Bellièvre to Nevers, 1 September 1593.

Father is held to be a good and prudent prince," he wrote to Nevers, "but from the news of your embassy to Rome, we judge our fear of the Spanish party . . . to be just." [54] Little progress was being made in the peace negotiations, he reported, although the nobility and the people were exhausted by the long wars.

Following the conference at Poissy, Henry IV, in a last gesture of conciliation, dispatched Bellièvre to the Duke of Mayenne to arrange for an extension of the truce and to hasten the sending of a representative of the League to Rome, where the Duke of Nevers awaited the commencement of negotiations with Clement VIII. Upon the completion of his mission, Bellièvre journeyed to Dieppe to report to the King, whom he found willing to prolong the truce until the position of the papacy was clarified.[55] In the end, the flurry of diplomatic activity which had engaged Bellièvre from the early summer of 1593 came to nothing. On December 27 the King revoked the truce "which his enemies had used to bring foreigners into the kingdom who perpetuated the war and the miseries of the people." [56] The Duke of Mayenne, in turn, reopened hostilities in January 1594.

54. B.N., Ms. fr. 3987, fol. 21.
55. B.N., Ms. fr. 15575, fol. 106, Bellièvre to [?], November 1593.
56. Pierre L'Estoile, *Journal de L'Estoile pour le règne de Henri IV,* ed. Louis-Raymond Lefèvre (Paris, 1948), I, 339.

In the Service of Henry IV:

1594–1599

THE ABJURATION of the King in July 1593 marked the beginning of the decline of the League. With the recommencement of civil war the following January, the Duke of Mayenne found himself confronted by large-scale defections, peasant revolts, and the resurgence of royalist sentiment in his cities.[1] Henry IV, in turn, faced the difficult tasks of reducing the last stubborn remnants of opposition to his rule and of establishing royal authority in the reconquered provinces and cities. To operate the machinery of state and to meet the problems of reconstruction, the King required men experienced in affairs and capable of representing the interests and needs of the crown to the multifarious centers of power in the divided kingdom. He recruited such men primarily from among those who had begun their careers in the service of the Valois monarchs.

By the spring of 1594, when he undertook his first major assignment

1. Henri Drouot, *Mayenne et la bourgogne: étude sur la ligue* (Paris, 1937), II, 273–97.

for Henry IV as intendant of Lyonnais, Bellièvre had fully regained the position and powers lost in the palace revolution of 1588. Undoubtedly his role as royalist spokesman during the first years of the King's reign was an important factor in his reappointment as councillor of state. Yet Henry counted leaguers as well as loyalists among his leading advisers. There was, in fact, only a limited pool of trained administrative and political talent in the country, and the King necessarily built upon the foundations of the Medicean administrative system.

In Bellièvre, the King gained a servant equally experienced in diplomacy, finance, and court politics. During his first five years in the service of Henry IV, the royal councillor performed a variety of functions in each of these fields. At once loyal to the crown and acutely sensitive to the pride and place of the great nobles, he was one of the principal agents charged with the pacification of the kingdom. Initially, his duties carried Bellièvre to Lyons, where he sought to impose his master's rule upon the city which had been the locus of his family's power.

II

NO MORE IMPORTANT VICTORY was won by the King in the final stage of the civil war than the submission of Lyons in February 1594. To reassert his authority in the regions of Lyonnais, Forez, and Beaujolais, Henry IV dispatched Bellièvre to Lyons as his personal representative with full powers in all matters of justice, finance, and police.[2] The councillor's service in Lyons and Lyonnais is of particular importance as an example of the early history of one of the principal institutions of the absolutist state. The development of the intendancy is generally and correctly associated with the internal policies of Cardinal Richelieu. However, its origins may be traced back to the mid-sixteenth century. At least from the time of Henry II's reign, the sending of *maîtres des requêtes* on extended missions into the provinces had become a general practice.[3] The struggle with the League accelerated the evolution of the intendancy, for

2. *Lettres inédites du Roi Henri IV au Chancelier de Bellièvre,* ed. E. Halphen (Paris, 1872), p. 69. (Hereafter cited as *Lettres inédites.*)
3. Gabriel Hanotaux, *Origines de l'institution des intendants des provinces* (Paris, 1884), pp. 17–50.

Henry IV, to a greater extent than his predecessors, relied upon these specially commissioned field administrators to pacify the realm.[4] Although the institution was not stabilized until the time of Richelieu, the late sixteenth century was important in its formation. In the hands of experienced crown servants, such as Bellièvre, the intendancy proved to be an effective instrument of pacification and a necessary counterweight to the power of the great nobles in the provinces.

When Bellièvre arrived in Lyons in June 1594, the chief royal official there was the military governor, Alphonse Ornano, whose troops had gained the city in February. Prior to Ornano's entry, Lyons had been a stronghold of the League under the governorship of Mayenne's high-handed brother, the Duke of Nemours. In September 1593, the notables of Lyons, aided by a popular uprising, placed Nemours under house arrest and turned the government of the city over to the archbishop, Pierre d'Epinac. This division among the leaders of the League and the continuing disorders in the city allowed a royalist minority to seize certain fortifications on the night of February 7. Within a day, royalist troops entered Lyons, and the assembly of notables declared its submission to Henry IV. Between February and June, civil government in Lyons was virtually suspended. Epinac, at Ornano's command, retired into exile, and the legal powers of government were transferred to the city's councillors, the *échevins*.[5] The capitulation of Lyons heightened partisan passions in the city, and a renewal of the civil conflict appeared imminent. In the face of these disorders and the continuing threat of an invasion by the Duke of Mayenne, Ornano was ordered by the King to remain in Lyons, and he exercised control of the government until the arrival of Bellièvre.[6]

The problems confronting the crown in Lyons and the surrounding countryside were outlined for the King in an undated and unsigned memorandum undoubtedly presented before Bellièvre's departure for the

---

4. Roger Doucet, *Les Institutions de la France au XVIᵉ siècle* (Paris, 1948), I, 424–33; Georges Pagès, "L'Evolution des institutions administratives du commencement du XVIᵉ siècle à la fin du XVIIᵉ," *Revue d'histoire moderne*, VII (1932), 40.

5. A. Kleinclausz, *Histoire de Lyon* (Lyons, 1939), I, 455–61. (Hereafter cited as Kleinclausz, *Lyon*.)

6. *Recueil des lettres missives de Henri IV*, ed. Berger de Xivrey (Paris, 1848), IV, 149. (Hereafter cited as *Lettres missives*.)

city.[7] In his introductory remarks to a series of proposals regarding the pacification of Lyons, the author of the memorandum claimed that a preponderant number of the inhabitants had remained loyal to the League after the submission of the notables. To overcome the "confusion, disorder, malice, and ignorance" which were present in Lyons, the memorandum recommended a purge of the leaguers, the posting of loyal troops, and the re-establishment of royalists in the principal offices. In addition, tight control was to be exercised over the election of the *échevins,* because "On them depend the peace and security of the city." Finally, the King was urged to dispatch *commissaires en la justice* to bring order to the city.

To the degree that they were implemented, these proposals comprised a veritable revolution in the civil government of Lyons and the definitive abridgement of that proud city's ancient liberties. As Sébastien Charléty has written, "The defeat of the League weighed on the city. Not only did it lose what remained of its independence, but it gained a new master, the intendant."[8] In its first intendant, however, Lyons found a benign master. The appointment of Bellièvre to bring Lyons under royal control and to restore civil government was a politic move on the part of Henry IV, suggesting that the King's aims were practical and conciliatory rather than punitive. Bellièvre was, of course, well known in the city, and certain of his relatives, notably Nicolas de Lange, occupied high positions there. Undoubtedly, the councillor's prestige and influence in Lyons facilitated the task of imposing royal authority upon his birthplace. At the same time, his standing at court allowed him to intercede on behalf of the *lyonnais.*[9]

The conditions in Lyons and the surrounding regions were chaotic when Bellièvre arrived to take up his duties. The army of the Marquis de Saint-Sorlin threatened the city, and foreign troops were in the area. While enemy troops ravaged the lands around Lyons, the small royalist garrison was powerless to act. Bellièvre found few economic resources available to him, because the governors and military chiefs, both royalist

---

7. B.N., Ms. fr. 16661, fols. 422–25.

8. *Histoire de Lyon depuis les origines jusqu'à nos jours* (Lyons, 1903), p. 114.

9. "Discours de Monsieur de Bellièvre sur la reduction de la ville de Lyon en l'obeissant du roi," B.N., Ms. fr. 15912, fols. 265–70.

and leaguer, monopolized the collection of taxes and diverted these revenues from the royal treasury into their own war chests.[10] Before the intendant could begin to resolve these problems, however, he was confronted with a serious challenge to his authority from Ornano.

In a letter to the *échevins* of Lyons, written in June 1594, Henry IV had delimited the spheres of activity of his two principal representatives in Lyonnais: "In military matters, I have given responsibility to Sieur d'Ornano, my lieutenant general in Dauphiné; and for other affairs, such as justice, police, and finance, I have granted authority to Sieur de Bellièvre, a leading figure in my Conseil d'état." [11] It is clear that the King intended a separation of the jurisdictions of his military and civil authorities. This distinction was emphasized by his sending a councillor of Bellièvre's stature and prestige, who, in Henry's words, "is well known as one of the most skilled and experienced personages in the kingdom and one of my closest advisers."

Despite the King's precisely stated intentions concerning the division of authority in Lyonnais, Ornano found cause to complain about the intendant's power. His protest elicited the following response from Henry IV: [12]

> I have seen your letter of June 25 and the complaint you have made of the power which I gave to Sieur de Bellièvre. . . . You have no cause to take offense at the aforesaid power, because it does not touch upon the authority which I have granted you. . . . I gave this task to . . . Bellièvre, even though his presence here was useful and necessary . . . because I believed he could serve well in those weighty affairs pertaining to Lyons and the neighboring provinces. . . . His reputation for honesty and his ability are recognized throughout my kingdom . . . and there is not a prince who would not defer willingly to his counsel. . . . You must not interfere in these matters of finance and justice which I have entrusted to him.

Thus, in matters vital to the reconstruction of his kingdom, such as financial administration and the regulation of the officers in Lyonnais, Henry limited the powers of his military commander and imposed his

10. "Lettre inédite de M. de Bellièvre au Roi Henri IV au sujet de l'emprisonnement du Duc de Nemours," *Revue du lyonnais* XVI (1858), 83.

11. *Lettres missives*, IX, 397–99.

12. *Ibid.*, pp. 398–99.

personal control through the intendant. This was an extraordinary act, however, and did not reflect any coherent plan of monarchical centralization at the expense of the governors and lieutenants general.[13] The great authority with which Bellièvre was invested represented Henry's response to the particular conditions in Lyons, Lyonnais, and the south generally, and was, moreover, a tribute to Bellièvre's high standing at court.

As intendant, Bellièvre was not simply a field administrator but also the principal political agent of the crown. In this latter capacity, he conducted the King's relations with the mighty proconsuls of the south, both leaguer and royalist, among whom Ornano was the least important. No small part of the intendant's time was devoted to that endless process of bargaining, bribing, and cajoling which constituted the internal diplomacy between King and overmighty subject.

Immediately after his arrival in Lyons, Bellièvre undertook negotiations with one such personage, the Duke of Nemours.[14] Although imprisoned, the Duke still commanded the loyalty of many of the citizens, and his troops held certain key cities and fortified places in the neighboring provinces. The object of Bellièvre's negotiations with Nemours was to extract an oath of allegiance to Henry IV. Nemours rejected the intendant's overtures but, after a month of discussions, agreed to turn over the fortified places occupied by his followers in return for his release from prison. He refused, however, to take an oath of loyalty to the King until his release. Nor would he negotiate the surrender of Vienne, contending that his brother Saint-Sorlin controlled the city. Bellièvre declined to conclude an agreement on Nemours' terms, and late in July he wrote to the King for further instructions. Before Henry had the opportunity to reply, the Duke escaped from prison, much to the consternation of the royal officials in Lyons.

Nemours' flight intensified the confusion in Lyons and threatened to undermine Bellièvre's mission of pacification. Although the city appeared determined to resist the King's enemies, the intendant feared an uprising by the partisans of Nemours and anticipated an alliance between the

13. Doucet, *Institutions*, I, 434.
14. "Lettres inédites de M. de Bellièvre au Roi Henri IV au sujet de l'emprisonnement du Duc de Nemours," *Revue du lyonnais*, XVII (1858), 308–16. (Hereafter cited as "L'Emprisonnement de Nemours.")

Duke and the Spanish King. Having lost the upper hand in his negotiations with Nemours, Bellièvre vainly sought to hold the Duke to the agreements he had signed while incarcerated. Nemours claimed that he had agreed to surrender the fortified places in order to gain his release from prison, but that since he had secured his liberty through God's grace and not the King's his earlier promises were nullified. To combat Nemours, who boasted that he would soon have 8,000 troops in the field, Bellièvre and Ornano sought to rally the governors of the nearby provinces to the defense of the south. At the same time, Bellièvre urged Henry IV to journey to the beleaguered city to raise the morale of the *lyonnais*.

The fiasco of the Duke of Nemours' evasion and the initial failure of Bellièvre's diplomatic effort undercut one of the principal objectives of royal policy—to secure a truce for the province of Lyonnais. Apparently fearing for his official life, Bellièvre deftly placed the blame for the escape on his antagonist, Ornano, and the *échevins* of Lyons.[15] Henry assured Bellièvre that he would not be held responsible for the incident and urged him to muster all of his strength for the struggle to preserve Lyonnais from the League.[16]

Although Bellièvre's primary center of activity lay in Lyonnais, where Nemours and Ornano held sway, his conciliatory mission involved him in the affairs of Provence, the preserve of yet another undisciplined proconsul, the Duke of Epernon. Epernon was independent both of the crown and of the League, and desired to establish his personal rule in Provence. At the King's command, Bellièvre sought to calm the impetuous Epernon in order to avoid an open conflict in Provence and to prevent an alliance of convenience between the Duke and the Spaniards.[17] The intendant's initial intervention with Epernon and his allies in the Parlement of Aix, in October 1594, was designed to gain an extension of an uneasy truce which had been established between the constable, Henri de Montmorency, and the Duke.[18] By March 1595, however, the truce had broken down. The Constable informed Bellièvre that Epernon's demands upon the crown were exorbitant and that the rebels in Provence had extended

15. B.N., Ms. fr. 15912, fol. 48, Bellièvre to Revol, 7 September 1594.
16. *Lettres missives,* IX, 403.
17. B.N., Fonds Dupuy 64, fol. 40, Bellièvre to Henry IV, 1 November 1594.
18. *Ibid.,* fol. 23, Bellièvre to Henry IV, October 1594.

81

the area under their control.[19] At about this time, Bellièvre exhorted the Duke to obedience: "Justice will not allow those who, through cupidity and impatience, bring ruin to their country to live long on this earth without great and exemplary punishment." Governorships, Bellièvre insisted, were dispensed at the will of the King and were not obtained by right of conquest. In his appeal to Epernon, Bellièvre reverted to his familiar arguments on the rights of kings and the duties of crown servants: [20]

> The prince owes us our preservation, and our services deserve to be rewarded. We owe service, fidelity, and obedience to our King. . . . The experience of the past and the great evils which we have suffered because some desired to introduce changes in the state teach us . . . to remain firm in the obedience we owe our King, outside of which, as we all know, there is no safety.

Thus, Bellièvre confronted the pretensions of the rebellious feudatory with the practical homilies of the *politique* and crown servant. Exhortation, however, was balanced by bribery, and Bellièvre softened his condemnation of Epernon's claim to the governorship of Provence by offering the Duke a generous pension, as well as the governments of Angoulême, Saintonge, and Poitou. In the end Epernon proved tractable, and the negotiations begun by the intendant were successfully concluded by another of the King's men, Pierre Forget de Fresne, to whom Henry IV delegated the responsibility for the affairs of Provence in March 1595.[21]

Bellièvre collaborated with Montmorency, the most powerful of the southern potentates, in the general pacification of the Midi and Provence. The Constable, as first officer of the crown, had paramount responsibility for the military operations, and, by the King's order, the intendant had recourse to him in matters relating to the defense of Lyons.[22] Bellièvre, in turn, served as liaison between Montmorency and the court. On at least one occasion Bellièvre intervened with the King to protect the Constable's interests. Regarding certain unspecified rumors circulating at the court, he wrote, "I believe that your service requires that those in your

19. B.N., Ms. fr. 15893, fol. 240, Bellièvre to Henry IV, 1 April 1595.
20. B.N., Ms. fr. 3952, fols. 344–48.
21. *Lettres inédites*, p. 164.
22. B.N., Ms. fr. 3547, fol. 32, Bellièvre to Montmorency, August 1594.

court cease talking about the first officer of the crown."[23] The unstable political situation in the south, he added, made the conciliation of Montmorency a necessity. Displaying his usual sensitivity to the interests of the great nobles, Bellièvre worked harmoniously with the Constable in the defense of the south.

Throughout the period of his intendancy, Bellièvre, with Montmorency's support, sought to focus the King's attention on the southern provinces. From the time of his arrival in Lyons, he insisted that only Henry's presence could preserve Lyonnais from the League and its Spanish allies.[24] In September 1594, the intendant issued the following warning to the King: "If your voyage is delayed any longer, there will be no hope that your servants can hold out. Your enemies, who are spreading the rumor that . . . Your Majesty cannot depart from Picardy, will be fortified in their evil designs."[25] The uncertainty over Henry's plans, Bellièvre continued, deterred many from joining the royalist forces. The King replied that it was impossible to depart from Picardy until the pacification of that province was completed. Even when free to attend to the affairs of the Midi, Henry reported that a lack of money and troops delayed his progress southward. As the year came to an end, he still remained in Picardy where, he wrote to Bellièvre, 20,000 enemy soldiers were gathered, "Who only await my leaving before invading this kingdom."[26]

During the last months of 1594, the tone of Bellièvre's letters became increasingly urgent, as he sent the King reports on threatening troop movements in Dauphiné, Piedmont, and Burgundy. Early in November, Bellièvre informed Henry that the Constable of Castille had crossed the Alps into Piedmont with 17,000 men. The linking of Castille's forces with those of the Dukes of Nemours and Mayenne placed Lyons and Lyonnais in a desperate situation. "The city of Cambrai is of great importance to your kingdom," Bellièvre wrote the King at this time, "but the city of Lyons, which can only be saved by your coming, gives you

23. B.N., Fonds Dupuy 64, fol. 21, Bellièvre to Henry IV, 29 September 1594.
24. See, for example, "L'Emprisonnement de Nemours," p. 310.
25. B.N., Fonds Dupuy 64, fol. 22, Bellièvre to Henry IV, 29 September 1594.
26. *Lettres inédites,* pp. 91–92, 101, 123.

control of a third of your realm." [27] Later in the month, the intendant informed Nevers that Mayenne and Nemours, supported by the Duke of Savoy, were planning a concerted attack upon Lyons.[28] Also, a rumor had reached the city in October that Andrea Doria's Spanish and Neapolitan troops were preparing to join forces with the League.[29] The penetration of Spanish soldiers into the Rhone valley and the imminent juncture of the foreigners with the armies of the rebellious dukes demoralized the royalists in Lyonnais. Bellièvre estimated, in September, that the garrison of Lyons numbered only 600 to 700 men.[30] Montmorency, meanwhile, had committed his forces to the siege of Vienne and was unable to offer Lyons protection. Bellièvre doubted that his city could survive the winter, for, as he wrote to the Duke of Nevers, the deterioration of the military situation in the neighboring provinces had caused the inhabitants of Lyons to lose heart.[31] Late in November, he reported, "We are about to see a war of religion in these parts." [32]

The fall of Buqueras in November and rumors of a vast influx of Spanish and Neapolitan troops only served to increase Bellièvre's pessimism concerning the fate of Lyons. "If only the King had arrived six weeks or a month ago," he lamented to Nevers, "Buqueras could have been saved and the siege of Vienne finished." [33] Because of the victories of the League and its allies, antiroyalist propaganda found a ready reception in Lyons. In order to protect the city and guard against a popular uprising, Bellièvre called for a regiment of Swiss mercenaries.[34] To Villeroy, now returned to the service of the crown, he repeated his warning that Lyons was on the verge of civil war: [35]

> I have learned that a letter which I wrote to you . . . has been inter-
> cepted. . . . It is, as always, on the same subject. The hope of your aid
> diminishes as the need for it increases. . . . The enemy is now master
> of the countryside. . . . I see that all the advice which I have given

27. B.N., Fonds Dupuy 64, fol. 40, Bellièvre to Henry IV, 1 November 1594.
28. B.N., Ms. fr. 3622, fol. 147. Bellièvre to Nevers, 27 November 1594.
29. B.N., Fonds Dupuy 64, fol. 33, Bellièvre to Henry IV, October 1594.
30. B.N., Ms. fr. 15912, fol. 42, Bellièvre to Henry IV, 7 September 1594.
31. B.N., Ms. fr. 3622, fol. 121, Bellièvre to Nevers, September 1594.
32. *Ibid.*, fol. 147, Bellièvre to Nevers, 27 November 1594.
33. *Ibid.*, fol. 137, Bellièvre to Nevers, 10 November 1594.
34. B.N., Ms. fr. 23195, fol. 141, Bellièvre to Henry IV, December 1594.
35. B.N., Ms. fr. 15893, fol. 201, Bellièvre to Villeroy, December 1594.

only serves to make me appear tiresome. . . . I no longer dare to write about those affairs, since they find it unreasonable when I warn that we fear a renewal of religious war here; nevertheless it seems that we are on the verge of it. . . . Marshal Biron must bring his forces to our aid.

The seriousness of the crisis in Lyonnais diminished somewhat during the first months of 1595, and an uneasy truce prevailed in Dauphiné. Despite Bellièvre's pleas, Henry IV chose to concentrate his forces in Burgundy, and it was there that the final scenes of the religious wars took place.[36] Henry did not enter Lyons until September 1595, only days before the capitulation of the Duke of Mayenne. The intendant's efforts to entice the King away from Picardy were not, however, entirely in vain. Henry gave some heed to the warnings from Bellièvre and other royalist leaders in the south that the principal danger to his realm derived from the presence of Spanish troops in Piedmont, Lyonnais, and Burgundy. In November 1594, the King had informed Bellièvre that Biron would soon be sent to Burgundy, and the Marshal was immediately instructed to proceed into that province and speed to the aid of Montmorency.[37] As Bellièvre impatiently awaited reinforcements, Biron lingered in Burgundy throughout the winter and spring of 1595. In March Bellièvre testily reminded Biron, engaged in the siege of Beaune, that Lyons was worth fifty such towns.[38] Nonetheless, the final campaign against the Duke of Mayenne demanded the presence of the bulk of the royal army in Burgundy, and Lyonnais remained on the periphery of the war zone until the conclusion of the struggle.

The crises of the war which raged around Lyonnais preoccupied the intendant throughout his tenure in office. Inevitably, the emergency limited the effectiveness of Bellièvre's efforts at reform in the spheres of civil government, justice, and, particularly, finances. Within Lyons, the first tasks confronting Bellièvre were the restoration of order and the reorganization of the economy. Shortly after arriving in the city, he reported that the local tax collector was unable to furnish one hundred *écus* for the King's service.[39] The commerce of the once flourishing city was at a

36. The best short account of the campaign in Burgundy is to be found in Drouot, *Mayenne*, II, 385–428.
37. *Lettres inédites*, p. 123.
38. B.N., Ms. fr. 15893, fol. 231, Bellièvre to Biron, 7 March 1595.
39. "L'Emprisonnement de Nemours," p. 310.

standstill, and as a consequence customs revenues had dwindled. Some months later, Bellièvre informed the King that the cost of maintaining the garrison and paying the arrears owed the troops had risen to 174,000 *écus,* only a small portion of which had been collected by the royal financial officials. "This city," he wrote, "has been reduced to an extreme necessity . . . nor is it any longer possible to obtain money from the citizens, and it would not be in your service to undertake to constrain them. Not a single *denier* has been contributed to your treasury this year because of the poverty which the people suffer." [40]

In the face of this economic calamity and in order to provide for the garrison, Bellièvre was forced to take extraordinary measures. One of his first acts had been to reorganize the customs, a reform which, given the state of commerce in Lyons, could have furnished little additional revenue.[41] The meager income from ordinary taxation was supplemented by forced loans and, in February 1595, Bellièvre requested the right to utilize the confiscated property of certain leaguers to pay for the garrison.[42]

As intendant of Lyonnais, Forez, and Beaujolais, Bellièvre was required to furnish funds and provisions not only for the defense of Lyons but also for neighboring towns. On one occasion, the King commanded his intendant to provide for the garrisons of Feurs and Douzy. Again, in November 1594, Bellièvre was ordered to facilitate the work of a royal commission charged with raising supplies for the armies in Lyonnais and Burgundy. In June 1595 the King appealed to Bellièvre "to take care of the garrison of Montluet and to aid it with munitions and bread until I shall arrive there." [43]

The excessive burden placed upon the citizens of Lyons and the general economic dislocation resulting from the war prevented the intendant from undertaking any far-reaching reforms of the financial structure. When Henry IV finally reached Lyons, in September 1595, economic anarchy still prevailed in the city.[44] Yet certain accomplishments must be

40. B.N., Ms. fr. 15893, fol. 247, Bellièvre to Henry IV, 6 April 1595.
41. Maurice Pallasse, *La Sénéchaussée et siège présidial de Lyon pendant les guerres de religion* (Lyons, 1943), p. 397.
42. B.N., Fonds Dupuy 64, fol. 67, Bellièvre to Henry IV, 15 February 1595; Ms. fr. 15893, fol. 247, Bellièvre to Henry IV, 6 April 1595.
43. *Lettres inédites,* pp. 71, 128, 189.
44. Kleinclausz, *Lyon,* II, 3.

credited to Bellièvre. Through a variety of expedients, he had managed to maintain the garrison during the crisis. Moreover, he successfully intervened with the King to prevent the complete despoliation of the wealth of the city.[45] He secured a guarantee from Henry that the funds in the royal treasury of Lyons would be used only in Lyonnais and would not be distributed throughout the kingdom.[46] Although his primary obligation was to the crown, Bellièvre in this instance served the interests of the region under his government as well.

The debilitating effects of the economic crisis in Lyons were compounded by the continuation of civil disorder. In his letters to the King, Bellièvre constantly stressed the fundamental loyalty of the *lyonnais* to the crown. Sentiment favorable to the League, however, remained strong in the city and reached a climax in February 1595 when a plot to deliver the city to the Duke of Nemours was discovered. Bellièvre, who exercised general supervision over police and justice, brought the conspirators to trial and reported that, after torture, exemplary punishment had been meted out to the principal leaders.[47] The intendant also watched carefully the activities of the Church in Lyons. In January 1595 he intervened to prohibit the publication of a papal edict granting a plenary indulgence to the citizens of the city. The edict, he reported to the King, cast doubt upon the validity of Henry's absolution.[48]

In addition to his police and censorial functions, Bellièvre oversaw the most minute aspects of local government.[49] Often it fell to the intendant to verify the loyalty of former leaguers who had been deprived of their civil rights and property after the surrender of Lyons. Such was the case of the councillor Regnault, whose liberties the King restored after an investigation by Bellièvre and the *échevins*. On other occasions, the King ordered Bellièvre to look into the circumstances behind the expulsion of two notables, Malezieux and Boisson, and to arrange for their return from exile if their punishments were unjust. Of a different nature was Henry's

---

45. B.N., Ms. fr. 15576, fol. 76, Bellièvre to Henry IV, March 1595; Ms. fr. 15893, fol. 247, Bellièvre to Henry IV, 6 April 1595.

46. *Lettres inédites*, p. 167.

47. B.N., Fonds Dupuy 64, fols. 64, 67, Bellièvre to Henry IV, 15, 17 February 1595.

48. B.N., Ms. fr. 15893, fol. 212, Bellièvre to Henry IV, 7 January 1595.

49. *Lettres inédites*, pp. 76, 95–96, 108, 179.

request that the intendant investigate the glass manufacturing industry in Lyons and advise on the granting of a monopoly to a Monsieur Sacrado. Each of these incidents, however minor, points up the fact that with the coming of the intendant even the most remote matters of government in Lyons were subject to the scrutiny of a high royal official. The important business of granting monopolies, pensions, and pardons now was in the control of Bellièvre and not of Ornano.

The only significant change effected by Bellièvre during the course of his intendancy was the reformation of the ancient governing body of Lyons and the original source of his family's power, the *Consulat.* Late in 1594, Bellièvre had intervened in the political affairs of the city to postpone the election of *échevins* for the following year. An election, he warned the King, would deepen the existing divisions in Lyons and harm the service of the crown.[50] The masters of the corporations, in turn, were advised to await the arrival of the King before proceeding to elect a new government. Before Henry's entry into the city, Bellièvre submitted a proposal for the reorganization of the municipal government which took form in the edict of Chauny of December 1595. Only a single piece of evidence remains establishing the intendant's responsibility for this edict. On December 8, the King wrote to Bellièvre, "I have followed your advice regarding the reformation of the *échevinage* of Lyons. I have expedited my letters patent in the form of an edict which I am sending you." [51]

It is not a little ironic that the son of one of the city's great families was, in large part at least, responsible for an act which diminished the authority of the *échevins* and thereby undermined the most precious of Lyons' liberties—the right of autonomous government. By the edict of Chauny, Henry IV imposed upon Lyons a prevotal system of government which corresponded to the municipal council of Paris.[52] The number of councillors was reduced to four, who were presided over by a *prévôt des marchands.* Although the councillors were elected as before and the

50. B.N., Ms. fr. 23195, fols. 147–48, 247, Bellièvre to Henry IV, December 1594.
51. *Lettres inédites,* p. 198.
52. Eugène Courbis, *La Municipalité lyonnaise sous l'ancien régime* (Lyons, 1900), pp. 88–91.

privileges of the city were theoretically retained, the reform of the municipal governing body opened the way to greater monarchical interference
in the administration of local affairs. As one great historian of the city has
written, "The reduction of the number of *échevins* was the means by
which centralization was reinforced." [53]

Sometime before the proclamation of the edict of Chauny, Bellièvre
departed from Lyons to resume his duties as councillor of state and of
finances. No lasting reforms, aside from the establishment of the prevotal
regime, were accomplished during his tenure. By and large, his mission
was a holding action, designed to keep the city in the King's camp until
the Midi had been pacified. Consequently, the intendant devoted his
primary efforts to matters of defense and supply, police, and the political
affairs of the overmighty subjects. Quite naturally, during the civil war
the activities of the field administrators were closely coordinated with
military operations, and political matters took precedence over reconstruction. The task of bringing Lyons under royal control would be taken up
by a succession of intendants who began to reside in the city in 1597.
Bellièvre's intendancy represented but a preliminary stage in the long
process of royal centralization. When Bellièvre left Lyons in November
1595, the intendancy had not been established as a permanent institution,
and the control of the city reverted to a military governor, the royal
bastard Vendôme.

III

UPON HIS RETURN TO PARIS, Bellièvre found himself again involved in
the wide range of political and economic problems which beset the
crown. Only a few weeks remained of the civil war which had ravaged
France for over three decades. With domestic strife reduced and the hopes
of the *politiques* at last fulfilled, the King and his servants turned to the
immense task of reconstructing a country overcome by poverty, dissen-
sion, and widespread corruption.

At the highest level, responsibility for advising the King and adminis-
tering his affairs was distributed among a small number of councillors
and secretaries who composed the *Conseil d'affaires*. Among them were

53. Kleinclausz, *Lyon*, II, 5.

the old intimates of Catherine de Medici—Bellièvre, Villeroy, and Cheverny—and younger men who had entered the service of the Valois monarchy at a later date.

The former chancellor, Philippe Hurault, Count of Cheverny, was the first of the high administrators dismissed by Henry III to return to the service of the monarchy. Despite his loyalty to the house of Lorraine, which had promoted his career, and misgivings concerning the future of the French crown, Cheverny chose to serve "the King whom God had given me as master by true and legitimate succession." [54] Through intermediaries at court, Cheverny informed the King of his desire to resume his duties as chancellor. In August 1590, Henry IV recalled Cheverny and restored to him the seals of his former office.

Both Cheverny and his successor in the chancellorship, Bellièvre, had passed their years of exile from the court on their estates. Villeroy, on the other hand, joined forces with the rebellious Duke of Mayenne and the League several weeks before the assassination of Henry III at Saint-Cloud. After his desertion from the royal house, Villeroy played an equivocal role in French politics. Although a leaguer, he maintained his connections with the royalist and neutralist elements in the country and served as the principal negotiator of the League.[55] During the years of his association with Mayenne, Villeroy constantly sought to frustrate the more ardent spirits in the Catholic party by advocating conciliatory and moderate policies. Indeed, the political ideas which he publicly proclaimed did not differ fundamentally from those of his colleague and fellow moderate, Bellièvre. Toward the end of 1589, a political tract of Villeroy's, "Avis d'état sur les affaires de ce temps," circulated in Paris.[56] In this pamphlet, the former secretary of state urged upon his master, Mayenne, a policy of reconciliation with the new king—a reconciliation predicated upon Navarre's conversion. Like Bellièvre, Villeroy publicly opposed the intrusion

54. Philippe Hurault, "Mémoires de Messire Philippe Hurault, Comte de Cheverny," *Collection complète des mémoires relatifs à l'histoire de France*, ed. M. Petitot (Paris, 1823), XXXVI, 166–67.

55. J. Nouaillac, *Villeroy, secrétaire d'état et ministre de Charles IX, Henri III et Henri IV* (Paris, 1909), pp. 156–57, 159–264.

56. Pierre L'Estoile, *Journal de L'Estoile pour le règne de Henri IV*, ed. Louis-Raymond Lefèvre (Paris, 1948), I, 31.

of foreign powers into French politics. He warned Mayenne of the dangers of a Spanish alliance, and, before the Estates of the League in 1593, he again raised the specter of Spanish domination of France.[57]

The conversion of Henry IV allowed moderate, prudent, and opportunistic members of the League, such as Villeroy, to disengage themselves from the service of the Duke of Mayenne, whose fortunes were fast declining. In September 1594, Villeroy returned to the royal court, long the source of his family's fortune and power, and resumed the duties of secretary of state.[58] The protest of his enemies at court—among them Madame, the sister of the King—went unheeded. To the charges, not completely unfounded, that his secretary of state was an opportunist, a fanatic, and a supporter of Spain, Henry's response, according to L'Estoile, was that "No man in his kingdom was more necessary to the state." [59] As secretary, the experienced Villeroy conducted the correspondence with France's ambassadors abroad, oversaw generally the kingdom's relations with foreign powers, and shared in the direction of domestic policies as well.[60]

In addition to his principal administrators and advisers—Sully, Villeroy, and Bellièvre—Henry IV summoned to his court two magistrates, Pierre Jeannin and Nicolas Brulart de Sillery. Jeannin, a lawyer and member of the Parlement of Dijon, had served the Duke of Mayenne from 1578 and was his principal representative in the province of Burgundy throughout the final years of civil conflict. Although by temperament a moderate and a member of the anti-Spanish faction within the League, Jeannin remained loyal to his patron until the latter's reconciliation with Henry IV in 1596. Jeannin played a major role in the negotiations leading to the Treaty of Folembray, which established the conditions of Mayenne's capitulation, and it was only after the signing of the treaty that he took an oath of loyalty to the crown.[61] As had been true

57. Nicolas Villeroy, "Mémoires d'estat," *Collection complète des mémoires relatifs à l'histoire de France,* ed. M. Petitot (Paris, 1824), XXXVI, 384–416, 468–80.
58. Nouaillac, *Villeroy,* p. 265.
59. L'Estoile, *Journal,* I, 429.
60. Nouaillac, *Villeroy,* p. 266.
61. Drouot, *Mayenne,* I, 115–19; II, 81–87, 446–62.

in the case of Villeroy, Henry IV disregarded Jeannin's long and intimate association with the League and rewarded this brilliant lawyer and diplomat handsomely. "He had such confidence in me," wrote Jeannin, "that he made me a member of that small council to which he communicated his principal affairs." [62]

Another member of that small council, the *Conseil d'affaires,* was Nicolas Brulart de Sillery, who, unlike his closest colleagues in the high councils of Henry IV, had remained in the service of the crown throughout the turbulent years of civil war. Sillery, like Bellièvre, Cheverny, and Jeannin, commenced his career in the sovereign courts, succeeding to his father's offices in the Parlement of Paris. During the religious wars he participated in the negotiations between Henry III and Henry of Navarre, and in 1587 he was sent to the Swiss cantons as ambassador. He held this post until July 1595. Upon his return from Switzerland, Sillery purchased the office of president in the Parlement of Paris.[63] He continued, however, in his functions as councillor of state and diplomat.

By 1596 Henry IV had fashioned an experienced and versatile corps of administrators and advisers to aid him in the reconstruction of the kingdom and the reconciliation of the dissidents. Throughout his reign, the structure of government remained relatively fluid, and, at least until the ascendancy of Sully, administrative responsibility remained collegial in nature. Consequently, the high administrators and principal councillors acted as personal agents of the monarchy, applying their talents to a variety of tasks, rather than as bureaucratic ministers charged with responsibility in one particular area. Many of those who have been included in the *noblesse des grandes fonctions* of Henry IV not only served in the *Conseil d'état* and the more specialized organs of government but also represented the crown as field administrators and diplomats. As has been seen, Bellièvre, upon his return to public life, participated in the negotiations with the League and made his principal contribution to the pacification of the realm during eighteen months as intendant of Lyonnais. Before his appointment as chancellor, he and Sillery concluded the peace with Spain at Vervins. Bellièvre also served as confidant of the King and, for the greater part of his councillorship, carried a large share of the

---

62. "Discours apologétique," B.N., Ms. fr. 3712, fol. 48.
63. B.N., Coll. Clair. 754, fol. 348.

burden in financial administration. In the breadth of his experience and the range of his duties, Bellièvre was typical of the omnicompetent king's men of this prebureaucratic age upon whom the functioning of the state machine depended.

IV

THE COMING OF PEACE and the abatement of religious fanaticism altered in a fundamental way the political situation in France. Yet Henry IV confronted many of the problems which had beset his predecessors. The external threat to the kingdom's security persisted, for the capitulation of Mayenne in 1596 did not end the war with Spain. Nor had the King crushed the independent feudatories within his realm; he had merely appeased them. Consequently, the tension between the crown and the provincial potentates, which had characterized the reigns of the later Valois kings, continued. Financial disorder also remained a constant source of worry to the crown and the councillors. Finally, religious divisions still represented a threat to a stable state structure.

The divisions, both political and religious, which remained in the kingdom offered Bellièvre the opportunity to practice the art of compromise and conciliation of which he was a master. Although the relationship between King and councillor lacked the intimacy which had marked Bellièvre's association with Catherine de Medici, Henry IV entrusted to Bellièvre the most important affairs, concerning both foreign and domestic problems. The royal councillor, in turn, was the prudent crown servant who subordinated his own judgments to those of his master. Regarding a policy which he did not favor, Bellièvre once noted, "Princes are often moved by a divine inspiration which sometimes leads them to do that which we have not anticipated." [64] On another occasion, he wrote of the King to Villeroy, "In matters of state, our judgment must depend on his." [65]

Bellièvre brought to the affairs of Henry IV not only an intimate knowledge of the workings of the government but also a pragmatic and prudent political sense. This pragmatism, characteristic of the *politique,* is

64. B.N., Ms. fr. 15894, fol. 316, Bellièvre to [?], 23 July 1599.
65. B.N., Ms. fr. 15893, fol. 327, Bellièvre to Villeroy, 15 March 1596.

93

nowhere seen more clearly than in Bellièvre's attitude toward the continuing religious divisions which obstructed the King's attempts to pacify his realm. From Lyons, in February 1595, Bellièvre communicated to his master certain proposals concerning the appeasement of the Catholic and Protestant factions in France. He advised the King to consider "What the wisest philosophers have long taught us: that it is impossible to avoid sedition in a kingdom or a republic if men of worth find themselves rejected and without hope of succeeding through their blood and their virtue." [66] The loyalty of Protestants was, therefore, to be rewarded. There were, however, the interests of the majority to be taken into account. Many Catholics, Bellièvre warned, feared that the principal offices in the kingdom would be occupied by Huguenots. In order to dispel the apprehensions of the majority, he urged the King to set forth, in a public statement, the exact number and location of offices to be granted his Protestant subjects. What is noteworthy in this advice is the clearly expressed notion that self-interest governs politics and, one of Bellièvre's favorite themes, that the problems arising from the religious divisions in the state could be solved politically if the interests of the constituent parts of the kingdom were preserved. Of course, Henry IV needed no lessons in the politics of self-interest from his councillors. But men of the *politique* temperament proved to be useful instruments in healing the wounds incurred by the religious crisis.

V

AS LONG AS THE WAR with Spain continued, the fiscal needs of the monarchy remained the primary preoccupation of the royal councillors stationed in Paris. While engaged in the pacification of Lyons, Bellièvre had been informed by Henry IV of his appointment to a place on the *Conseil des finances,* which office he assumed upon his return to Paris.[67] The death of the superintendent of finances, François d'O, had allowed the King to reconstitute the *Conseil des finances* and to suppress the office of superintendent, which had been discredited by O's maladministration. In November 1594, Henry announced his intention of dividing authority

66. *Ibid.,* fols. 224–25.
67. *Lettres missives,* VI, 266–67.

in financial administration among nine of his most trusted councillors.[68] Initially, the *Conseil des finances* was composed of the Duke of Nevers, the Duke of Retz, Montmorency, Cheverny, Gaspard de Schomberg, and four administrative experts—Bellièvre, Nicolas Harlay de Sancy, Pierre Forget de Fresne, and Jacques de la Grange-Le-Roi. Fragmentary evidence on the work of the council suggests that it was the latter four members who carried the major burden of the King's finances. Sully, who would later gather the direction of financial affairs into his own hands, was not a member of the original council. The great financial minister did not enter the *Conseil des finances* until 1596, but within the span of a few years he came to dominate it and eventually replaced the collegial body as the effective controller of finances.[69]

The *Conseil des finances* was an instrument of the crown, responsive to the King's commands, and never exercised an independent authority in financial administration. It was more than merely an advisory body, however. As Henry's letters to Bellièvre during the years 1596 and 1597 indicate, the council was expected not only to advise the crown on financial affairs but also to raise the funds necessary for the military campaign against Spain.[70] In addition, it was charged, under the statute of November 1594, with the responsibility of drawing up an annual report on the financial state of the realm, the royal warrant concerning the levying of the *taille,* and a register of the offices sold by the monarchy.[71] The functions of the council were, therefore, threefold: to advise the King, to provide the monies for the royal war chest, and to rationalize the administration of finances. The fact that Henry IV soon reverted to a more centralized system suggests that the collegial body failed to satisfy the demands made upon it by the crown.[72]

Indeed, the problems confronting the *Conseil des finances* were formidable, and the conditions arising from the continuing struggle with Spain

68. B.N., Ms. fr. 16626, fols. 20–26.
69. *Inventaire des arrêts du Conseil d'état, règne de Henri IV,* ed. Noël Valois (Paris, 1886), I, lxx.
70. See, for example, *Lettres inédites,* pp. 203–19.
71. B.N., Ms. fr. 16626, fols. 20–26.
72. For a defense of the council of finances, see Albert Chamberland, "Le Conseil des finances en 1596 et 1597 et les economies royales," *Revue Henri IV,* I (1905–6), 20–32, 152–63, 250–60, 274–84.

precluded any wholesale reformation of the financial structure. Bellièvre, with his customary pessimism, looked upon the administration of finances as the most difficult burden in the kingdom. The royal debt, the extreme poverty of the people, and the widespread corruption among the crown's officials, he held, would frustrate any attempt to bring order to the financial affairs of France. "I believe that order in finances," he wrote, "depends upon the order or disorder in the other affairs of His Majesty. The question is, how can this order be established and how will it be preserved?" [73]

After his intendancy, Bellièvre appears to have devoted the greater part of his energies to fiscal problems. That he commanded the full confidence of the King, at least initially, cannot be doubted. On one occasion, Henry IV ordered him to use his own judgment in dealing with a question concerning the financial affairs of the clergy, because, "If you were here I would act in this entirely on your advice." [74] Thus, while the warrior King campaigned, Bellièvre and his colleagues worked desperately to raise funds both through ordinary channels and by extraordinary means. The dimensions of the problem were suggested in a letter written by Bellièvre and Sancy, which revealed that the councillors had found but two financiers prepared to negotiate a loan—and this at exorbitant rates. "It is difficult to avoid calumny from such contracts," the councillors explained, "but the state in which the King finds himself now overrides all other considerations." [75]

The process of filling the royal war chest was as much a political as an administrative operation. When doubling the *aides*, inducing the clergy to contribute its tenth, or withholding funds from the city of Paris, the King's government engaged in delicate bargaining sessions with the corporate institutions of the realm. As the principal link between the crown, the councils, and the constituted bodies in Paris, Bellièvre carried on a large part of these negotiations. The councillor's dealings with the clergy in the spring of 1596 are illustrative of this internal diplomacy.

73. B.N., Ms. fr. 3622, fols. 137, 142–43, Bellièvre to Nevers, 10, 18 November 1594.

74. *Lettres inédites,* p. 203.

75. B.N., Ms. fr. 3578, fol. 19, Bellièvre and Sancy to Montmorency, 30 November 1595.

Before demanding a subsidy from an assembly of the French Church, Bellièvre first sought to obtain from the King a conciliatory response to certain of the clergy's demands regarding the Huguenots. He and his colleagues in the council then proposed a plan by which lands alienated in the past would be restored to the Church. At the same time, Bellièvre held a series of meetings at his residence to adjust the differences between the clergy and the *Hôtel de Ville* of Paris—differences arising from the Church's delinquency in paying *rentes* owed the city. All of this, in turn, formed the background to the councillor's plea to the clergy for the continuation of the traditional ecclesiastical subvention.[76] The financiers also required careful handling. In May 1596 Henry wrote Bellièvre, "Use your credit and all you can apply in way of persuasion to dispose . . . Zamet and his friends to furnish what you expect of them in order to form the necessary sum."[77]

As one of the intermediaries between the crown and the various centers of wealth in the kingdom, Bellièvre eventually incurred the displeasure of Henry IV, whose letters revealed a certain impatience with the delays, excuses, and plaints of his councillors. Although Sully would, in his memoirs, accuse the *Conseil des finances* of incompetence and self-seeking, there is no evidence to substantiate his charges. There can be no doubt, however, that Henry was dissatisfied with the work of his council, despite Bellièvre's frequent protestations that "We labor as best we can to provide for the payment of his army, which is the most important matter in the kingdom."[78] As early as May 1596 the King indicated his impatience with the cautious Bellièvre. Concerning a forced loan which he intended to impose, Henry wrote, "I desire that your answer be in writing, and that it be purely and simply a yes or no, without entering into reasons and excuses. . . . I shall judge the degree of your affection by this."[79] A more serious crisis between crown and council erupted in the late summer of 1597, when the *Conseil des finances* found itself compelled to refute Henry's criticisms of its conduct by issuing a statement defending its

76. B.N., Ms. fr. 15893, fol. 328, Bellièvre to Villeroy, 15 March 1596; fols. 336–37, Bellièvre and Cheverny to Henry IV, 21 April 1596; fols. 311–15.
77. *Lettres inédites,* p. 207.
78. B.N., Ms. fr. 3547, fol. 18, Bellièvre to Montmorency, June 1596.
79. *Lettres inédites,* p. 212.

policies. This apology, which was probably drafted by Bellièvre,[80] followed closely the gloomy predictions he had set forth in his letter to the Duke of Nevers some years earlier. The failure of the *Conseil des finances* to produce the funds incessantly demanded by the King was attributed to the general dislocation, corruption, and poverty caused by the years of civil and foreign war, rather than to any lack of zeal or loyalty on the part of the councillors. The analysis of the financial problems of the kingdom, offered in self-defense by Bellièvre and his colleagues, was justified by later events. Their most severe critic, the Duke of Sully, did indeed restore the financial integrity of France, but only after a temporary peace with Spain had been achieved.

The imbroglio over the financing of the Spanish war in no way diminished Bellièvre's prestige, nor was he ever excluded from the financial affairs of the monarchy. As late as January 1599 we find Maurice of Hesse seeking Bellièvre's support in obtaining funds from Henry IV to combat Spanish intrusions into Westphalia. "Knowing the rank you hold and the credit you have with His Majesty," wrote the German Prince, "we wanted to ask you to advance this affair through your authority."[81] Royal officials, on missions in the provinces, and notables, both within and outside the kingdom, continued to seek his intervention with the King and councils in affairs which concerned them, particularly in the realm of finances and financial administration.

Together with his duties in the *Conseil des finances,* Bellièvre participated in the formulation of policy. Unfortunately, the nature and quality of his counsel lay, for the most part, hidden behind the formal language of official correspondence or submerged in the collective advice of the *Conseil d'affaires.* In matters of religion, for example, we know little of his attitude toward the most important legislation of the period, the Edict of Nantes. When announcing the edict to the Parlement of Paris, Henry IV claimed to have followed the advice of Bellièvre, Villeroy, Sillery, and others of the council.[82] Bellièvre, in turn, supported the edict as the only

80. Chamberland, "Le Conseil des finances," pp. 279–82. The document is reproduced by Chamberland.

81. B.N., Ms. fr. 15911, fol. 377, Maurice of Hesse to Bellièvre, 24 January 1599.

82. *Lettres missives,* V, 91.

means of preventing "a great explosion in the state," and he defended the King against his Catholic critics.[83] His precise contribution to the legislation, however, remains unclear. In foreign affairs, the councillor was among the moderates at court. Concerning the approval by the council of a treaty with England, Bellièvre, on behalf of his colleagues, urged prudence upon the King and warned that the country needed a respite from war.[84] Likewise, in his dealings with the constituted bodies of the realm, the councillor displayed a more conciliatory attitude than his master.[85] A product of Medicean politics, Bellièvre was ever the moderate, the conciliator, and the opponent of innovation.

The dynastic affairs of the monarchy—those family quarrels and marriage negotiations which were such an important part of early modern politics—were also the responsibility of the royal councillors. Early in 1596, for example, Henry called upon Bellièvre to intercede in a dispute between Queen Louise, the widow of Henry III, and the Duke of Mayenne. The Queen, supported by the Duchess of Angoulême, held Mayenne responsible for the assassination of her husband and sought to prevent, through a legal action, the verification in Parlement of the edict of peace between the crown and the house of Lorraine. Bellièvre was drawn into the affair when Queen Louise asked for his advice and aid. Fearful lest Louise's activities offend Mayenne and disrupt the precarious peace, Bellièvre protested the King's determination to avenge the murder of his cousin.[86] Henry ordered his councillor to communicate with the Queen's advisers and to arrange some solution which would content her and preserve the peace. Although the details of this negotiation are lacking, the success of Bellièvre's intervention may be presumed, for in March 1596 the King wrote his councillor thanking him for "facilitating the verification of the edict of my cousin, the Duke of Mayenne." [87]

83. B.N., Fonds Dupuy 322, fol. 57, Bellièvre to Pontcarré, n.d.
84. B.N., Ms. fr. 15893, fol. 351, Bellièvre to Henry IV, June 1596.
85. Albert Chamberland, *Le Conflit de 1597 entre Henri IV et le Parlement de Paris* (Paris, 1904), pp. 43–48. Chamberland has reproduced several memoranda drawn up by Bellièvre as a basis for a royal speech before the parlement. Bellièvre's drafts were far more conciliatory and temperate than the fiery address which was, in fact, given by the King.
86. B.N., Ms. fr. 15893, fol. 301, Bellièvre to Henry IV, February 1596.
87. *Lettres inédites*, pp. 199–201, 203–4.

A second episode, involving the dissolution of Henry's marriage to Marguerite of Valois, offers another illustration of Bellièvre's role in dynastic affairs.[88] In February 1598, while Bellièvre and Sillery were engaged in peacemaking at Vervins, the King revealed his intention of taking a new wife, "in order to gladden and console my people with the hope of seeing me with children." Henry instructed Bellièvre, who was something of an expert on the marital difficulties of the royal couple, to consult with the *éminence grise* of the peace conference, Alexander de Medici, papal legate to France, "on the path to take in order to manage it in a suitable manner." The legate was receptive to Bellièvre's overture, and late in March the King ordered his councillor to discuss with Medici the legal aspects of the proposed dissolution. In a final letter, Henry acknowledged the successful completion of these preliminary negotiations: "I have received your advice on the procuration which I have sent you, which I found very good and shall follow."

VI

THE CLIMAX OF BELLIÈVRE's CAREER as peacemaker came in 1598 when he and Sillery were selected by Henry IV to negotiate a treaty with the representatives of Philip II of Spain.[89] The first moves toward peace were begun in June 1597 under the auspices of the papacy. At that time, Bellièvre represented Henry IV in a series of meetings with the papal intermediaries, Alexander de Medici and a Franciscan general, Bonaventura Calatagirone. The Franciscan, recently returned from the Low Countries, reported to Bellièvre that Philip II and his governor in Brussels, the Cardinal-Archduke Albert, were prepared to treat for peace.[90] Ever the ardent advocate of peace, the royal councillor urged the King to respond positively to Philip's initiative. In a letter to Villeroy, Bellièvre revealed that several of the leading officers of the crown—Montmorency, Sillery, and Sancy—shared his opinion that "It is best to

88. *Ibid.*, pp. 232–33, 234, 235–36.
89. The most important documents relating to this negotiation are to be found in Pomponne de Bellièvre and Nicolas Brulart de Sillery, *Mémoires de Bellièvre et de Silleri*, 2 vols. (Amsterdam, 1696). (Hereafter cited as Bellièvre and Sillery, *Mémoires*.)
90. B.N., Ms. fr. 15893, fol. 451, Bellièvre to Henry IV, 30 June 1597.

enter into this negotiation immediately, for time may bring something which will . . . ruin all." [91] However, the King, suspicious of the role of the Franciscan general, hesitated to follow the advice of his more prudent advisers.[92] Throughout the summer, negotiations were interrupted while Henry undertook the siege of the city of Amiens. Bellièvre, forced to subordinate his desire for immediate negotiations to the policies of his master, continued to act as liaison between the crown and Alexander de Medici.[93] The deadlock between the King and the papal representatives, which arose from a controversy over the status of Amiens, was finally broken by the capitulation of that city to the French forces in September 1597. The end of the six months' siege found France and Spain exhausted and without the resources or manpower to go on with the struggle. Both sides were now prepared to accept the mediation of the Florentine cardinal.

In February 1598, the long and tortuous negotiations which would result in the peace of Vervins were begun.[94] On the third day of that month, Bellièvre and Sillery, having received their instructions and plenipotentiary powers from the King, left for Vervins, a town on the frontier of Picardy, where they were joined by Alexander de Medici and the deputies of Philip II, Jean Richardot and Jean-Baptiste de Taxis. In his instructions, Henry IV ordered the French ambassadors to work for two primary objectives—the restitution of certain towns and fortified places held by the Spaniards and the inclusion of France's allies, England and the United Provinces, within the terms of the treaty. An accord on the restitution of Calais and the occupied towns of Picardy and Brittany was signed by the ambassadors on March 24. The negotiations foundered, however, as the papal intermediaries and the ambassadors sought to resolve a conflict between Henry IV and Philip II's ally, Charles, Duke of Savoy. Bellièvre and Sillery informed the King that the negotiations were threatened by his quarrel with Savoy and urged him to accept the arbitration of the Pope. Henry's willingness to allow papal mediation on this

91. *Ibid.*, fol. 454, Bellièvre to Villeroy, 30 June 1597.
92. On the King's attitude, see *Lettres inédites*, pp. 221–29.
93. *Ibid.*, pp. 229–31.
94. Bellièvre and Sillery, *Mémoires*, I, 3, 35, 143–53, 154–64, 223–28, 234–37; II, 274–75.

issue permitted his deputies to deal with the final obstacle to peace, the participation of England and the United Provinces in the negotiations. More concerned with the conclusion of a peace with Spain than with the strict observance of the treaties of confederation between France and her allies, Bellièvre and Sillery pressed the King to disengage himself from his commitments to the alliance. This appeal coincided with the deterioration of France's relations with the Protestant powers. In a letter to his ambassadors at Vervins, Henry expressed his impatience with the delaying tactics of the English and commanded Bellièvre and Sillery to conclude the treaty with Spain as rapidly as possible. The ambassadors succeeded in negotiating a two months' cessation of hostilities between Spain and the United Provinces and England, and on May 2 the Treaty of Vervins was signed. In July, Bellièvre and Sillery, in the company of Biron, journeyed to Brussels to witness the ratification of the treaty by the Cardinal-Archduke Albert.[95]

The conclusion of the peace with Spain followed closely upon the proclamation of the Edict of Nantes in April 1598. These two events marked the end of the religious wars in France and the triumph of the policies of the *politiques*. As an agent of the monarchy, Bellièvre had contributed greatly to the pacification of the realm and the making of peace. As a councillor, believing firmly that the use of force was more detrimental to the state than the existence of two religions and that the right ordering of the kingdom depended upon peace, he had constantly urged upon the crown policies of compromise and conciliation. From Brussels he wrote the King, "To bring down his enemies is a source of greatness for a prince; but to be able to do good . . . for his friends and enemies is a more excellent and more desirable greatness." [96] Bellièvre's good prince was to be the arbiter of peace in Europe, and the treaty of Vervins was to be the means to this "more excellent greatness." If the Pope were disgusted by the Edict of Nantes, reconciliation with Spain would "soften his spirit." [97] It would also serve the ends of French statecraft by dividing the Hapsburgs. "We judge men by their interests," Bellièvre stated, and it appeared to him that the Cardinal-Archduke

95. B.N., Ms. fr. 15894, fol. 184.
96. *Ibid.*, fol. 137, Bellièvre to Henry IV, July 1598.
97. *Ibid.*, fol. 69, Bellièvre and Brulart to Villeroy, 7 April 1598.

Albert sought his own greatness and not that of the Spanish King.[98] To achieve higher ends, France had to adopt a more restrained attitude toward the Protestant powers. Of the Dutch he wrote, "These people . . . have a goal and to reach it they will sell both mother and father and even Jesus Christ." [99]

The triumph of diplomacy at Vervins represented the apogee of Bellièvre's career as a peacemaker among the warriors and earned him the profound, if not lasting, gratitude of Henry IV.[100] When the death of the Count of Cheverny in July 1599 left vacant one of the two highest offices in the kingdom, Henry rewarded his *premier et plus ancien conseiller d'état* with the chancellorship.

98. *Ibid.*, fol. 39, Bellièvre and Brulart to Villeroy, March 1598.
99. *Ibid.*, fol. 54, Bellièvre and Brulart to Villeroy, 26 March 1598.
100. *Lettres missives,* IV, 985–87.

His Majesty's Chancellor:

1599–1607

B ELLIÈVRE, THEN, IS CHANCELLOR." With these words, according to Pierre L'Estoile, Henry IV greeted the news of the death of the Count of Cheverny.[1] The years of Bellièvre's chancellorship both marked the height of his career as servant of the French monarchy and witnessed his decline into a powerless, cantankerous, and, if Sully is to be believed, senile ornament of the court of Henry IV. His high office endowed Bellièvre with great powers in the area of judicial administration and conferred upon him the politically important role of *chef du conseil*. The following pages are primarily concerned with these two aspects of the Chancellor's functions and with the struggle in the *Conseil d'état* which resulted in his displacement. First, however, it is necessary to examine the nature of the office as it had evolved during the sixteenth century.

The King's choice of his septuagenarian councillor to fill the most

1. *Journal de L'Estoile pour le règne de Henri IV,* ed. Louis-Raymond Lefèvre (Paris, 1948), I, 577.

exacting and important administrative post in the kingdom followed the tradition, well established by the sixteenth century, of appointing to the chancellorship eminent members of the *robe longue*.[2] From the time of Charles VIII, the office had been occupied, though not in unbroken succession, by a series of distinguished jurists, among whom were included Antoine Duprat, François Olivier, and Michel de L'Hôpital. Despite his age and infirmities, Bellièvre was, of all the royal councillors, best qualified by virtue of his legal training, his service in the sovereign courts, and his long experience in the councils to fill the office once held by the great *politique* L'Hôpital.

As chancellor, Bellièvre was "the magistrate of magistrates, the chief of justice and of all the affairs of the country."[3] He was numbered in that small group of officers, *les grands officiers de la couronne,* who held appointments for life, and who were considered to be instruments of the state and not the personal servants of the monarch. The powers attributed to the office of chancellor, which under the Carolingians and early Capetians had been confined to the supervision of the few bureaus centralized in the royal palace, were greatly augmented during the course of the early modern period. The extension of royal authority and the increasingly complex structure of government in France placed a greater burden upon the central administrative officer who served as an auxiliary to the king in all matters of finance, justice, and legislation. In the sixteenth century, Roger Doucet has written, "The chancellor became the chief of an administration dispersed throughout the length and breadth of the kingdom."[4]

The influence of the chancellor extended into all of the major administrative departments. As supervisor of the chancery and *garde des sceaux,* he was charged with the sealing of all royal edicts and ordinances. Control of the seals, in turn, gave him a limited check upon monarchical legislation. In the capacity of *chef du conseil*, the chancellor presided over the royal councils and exerted an important influence upon the formulation of legislation. In judicial affairs, he served not only as the principal

2. Roger Doucet, *Les Institutions de la France au XVIe siècle* (Paris, 1948), I, 104.

3. B.N., Ms. fr., nouv. acq. 9734, fol. 3.

4. Doucet, *Institutions*, I, 102–3, 105, 107.

administrator but also as the chief justice of the state with the privilege of presiding over Parlement. Finally, the chancellor acted as the primary spokesman of the crown before the constituted bodies of the kingdom.

This diversity of functions and the privileges attributed to the office bestowed upon a strong chancellor, such as L'Hôpital, the virtual powers of a prime minister. A distinction must be drawn, however, between the theoretical and real powers of the office. Cheverny, for example, was a far less important figure in the government of Henry IV than the principal councillors and secretaries of state. Likewise, Bellièvre's tenure in the chancellorship demonstrated that the actual prestige and influence of the office depended ultimately upon the King's good will rather than upon established tradition or juridical status. When Bellièvre took up his duties in August 1599, he commanded the full confidence of Henry IV and, consequently, exercised considerable authority in the government. In turn, a simple act of the King in 1605 deprived the Chancellor of much of his power, although he retained the office until his death in 1607.

II

ON AUGUST 2, 1599, royal letters granting Bellièvre the rights and privileges of the chancellorship were dispatched to all of the constituted bodies.[5] In his decree, Henry IV reviewed the career of his chancellor, particularly noting his role in the negotiating of the Treaty of Vervins. The King, after remarking on "the singular integrity" of Bellièvre, commanded his officers to render to the Chancellor the recognition and obedience owed to the crown itself. In his replies to the letters of tribute sent by the notables of the kingdom after Henry's pronouncement, Bellièvre, characteristically cautious and self-effacing, emphasized his age, infirmities, and feelings of impotence in face of the great burdens of his office. To Jacques Davy du Perron he lamented, "I confess that I feel too weak to combat the great number of monsters which our civil wars have introduced; the corruption which some have fomented, the weaknesses which others have tolerated."[6] In a letter to the Parlement of Paris, Bellièvre spoke of the chancellorship as "a position which I have not

5. A.N., P. 2339, fols. 759–63.
6. B.N., Fonds Dupuy 194, fol. 87ᵛ, Bellièvre to Du Perron, September 1599.

sought and which I realize surpasses my strength."[7] Once in office, however, he proved to be a resourceful and independent chancellor and a staunch defender of the integrity of the judicial system.

As chancellor, Bellièvre gave expression to a mode of thought which may best be described as constitutional. To his mind, custom, the old laws, and the traditional forms of a corporate order provided the indispensable framework for a stable society. On April 14, 1600, he went before the Parlement of Paris to appeal, in the name of the King, for the reform of the judicial system and for the return to an older, purer morality, which had existed before the civil conflict.[8] In this discourse, his first major pronouncement as chancellor, Bellièvre set forth with great clarity that notion of the primacy of law which was fundamental to his conception of the rightly ordered kingdom.

Following the customary praise of the monarch, the Chancellor turned the Parlement's attention to the problem of decay within the legal institutions of the country. A restoration of public order, he argued, depended not so much on the enactment of new statutes as on rigid adherence to the old laws. He warned that the greed and corruption of lawyers, the high cost of trials, malpractices on the part of local judicial officials, and nepotism within the sovereign courts threatened the integrity of the courts and the sanctity of the law, upon which orderly and equitable government were based. The King regarded justice as "the firmest pillar which undergirds the structure of his kingdom," the Chancellor stated, and upon the parlements and his office devolved the royal conscience in all matters pertaining to justice. Thus, it was the responsibility of the guardians of the law to restore the good customs of the past. The wickedness of the times demonstrated that "Our spirits always need some restraint, some corrective, which moderates them and contains them within the limits of duty and reason. . . . We must depend on the judgment of the law and not on the incertitude of men." This affirmation of the central position of the law in the state was followed by an appeal for obedience to the crown: "Render to His Majesty in all things the obedience which our fidelity obliges, and grant to no subject of this

---

7. Quoted in François Duchesne, *Histoire des chanceliers et gardes des sceaux de France* (Paris, 1680), pp. 689–90.
8. B.N., Ms. fr. 15894, fols. 388–91.

crown, whatever grandeur or dignity he possesses, the quality of a good man if he does not also demonstrate his faithfulness, devotion, and obedience to the king."

As a spokesman for the King and a loyal crown servant who had contributed significantly to the absolutist cause during the religious wars, Bellièvre naturally associated obedience to the crown with obedience to the law, which was, after all, the King's law. There remained, however, the question of the crown's relationship to the judiciary, to the laws, and to the customs of the country. Throughout the *ancien régime,* a tension existed between the monarchy, the fount of all law, and the guardians of that law and of the judicial process. An absolutist king, such as Henry IV, quite rightly regarded the law as his law, the courts as his courts, and did not hesitate to intervene in order to impose the royal will upon the judiciary. Bellièvre, on the other hand, was both an advocate of absolutism and a legist who placed great value upon process, the formalities of the judicial system, and the rights of the constituted bodies. On more than one occasion, the Chancellor was forced to remind his master that royal intervention in the judicial process undermined monarchical authority, which found its truest expression in the law.

For reasons of state or of equity, more often as a favor to some loyal follower or courtier, Henry IV frequently interfered with the workings of justice. The correspondence between the King and his Chancellor reveals innumerable examples of such intervention. Bellièvre, in turn, often imposed a temporary restraint upon royal actions which he considered arbitrary, detrimental to the equitable administration of justice, or opposed to the traditional rights of the sovereign courts. The Chancellor in no way denied the idea that sovereign power in matters of justice resided in the crown. He did seek, however, to resist the encroachments of the absolute monarchy upon the preserve of the judiciary and to restrict practices, such as the proliferation of officers and patents of nobility, which he regarded as harmful to the kingdom.

Something of the perpetual tensions between the crown and the Chancellor may be glimpsed in the following letter of Henry IV: [9]

9. *Recueil des lettres missives de Henri IV,* ed. Berger de Xivrey (Paris, 1876), IX, 58. (Hereafter cited as *Lettres missives.*)

I send you this note in my own hand to say that, all difficulties ceasing, you will no longer withhold the seals from the remission granted Sr. de Saint-Jour . . . as a thing I want and which I command you; and the same for the ennobling of Captain Beauregard, and the declaration of councillor Basset, and the abolition for the Dame de Saint-Auban.

As one encounters letter after letter in this tone, a pattern of obstructionism appears in Bellièvre's conduct of his office which can be explained neither by the institutional inertia of the chancery nor by the infirmities of the Chancellor. What, then, were the issues at stake in the frequent clashes between Henry IV and his loyal servant?

Most often it was the King's habit of exercising his personal justice which disturbed the Chancellor. A common form of royal intervention in the judicial process was the remission of penalties imposed by the courts of law. Henry IV, for example, frequently granted remissions to noblemen who had been brought to trial for killing their opponents in duels.[10] Assorted murderers, bankrupts, and minor malefactors also were the beneficiaries of the King's clemency,[11] while the great nobles of the kingdom often worked through the crown to preserve their clients from judicial punishment.[12] A second form of royal interference was the *évocation*—the transferal of a case from one jurisdiction to another. In October 1600 Henry directed the Chancellor to arrange for the removal of a case from the Parlement of Toulouse. "I know that you will say that such procedures are extraordinary," he wrote to Bellièvre, "but I prefer to be deficient in formalities rather than in justice."[13] At another time, the King, acting on behalf of the Duke of Biron, ordered Bellièvre to transfer a trial from a provincial *baillage* to the royal council.[14] In such cases,

---

10. See, for example, *Lettres inédites du Henri IV au Chancelier Bellièvre du 16 Mars au 28 Octobre 1604*, ed. E. Halphen (Paris, 1883), pp. 5, 79. (Hereafter cited as *Lettres inédites, 1604*). Also see *Lettres missives*, IX, 17–19.

11. *Lettres inédites du Henri IV au Chancelier Bellièvre, 1603*, ed. E. Halphen (Paris, 1883), p. 66. (Hereafter cited as *Lettres inédites, 1603*.) Also see *Lettres inédites, 1604*, p. 18; and *Lettres missives*, IX, 59.

12. *Lettres missives*, IX, 61; B.N., Ms. fr. 15897, fol. 520, Sully to Bellièvre, 25 September 1603.

13. *Lettres missives*, IX, 17.

14. *Lettres inédites du Roi Henri IV au Chancelier de Bellièvre*, ed. E. Halphen (Paris, 1872), p. 304. (Hereafter cited as *Lettres inédites.*)

involving the great lords of the kingdom or their clients, Henry occasionally demanded personal cognizance. Usually, however, these affairs were referred to the Great Council, the highest court of appeal in the kingdom. An excellent example of this type of *évocation* was the King's intervention in support of the Italian favorite of Marie de Medici, Rinuccini, who sought to remove a suit involving his three brothers from the jurisdiction of the Parlement of Dauphiné. "I know that the tendency of the law and justice requires that it be sent to the nearest parlement," Henry wrote to the Chancellor, "but . . . Rinuccini desires . . . that it be in my Great Council." [15] The King then commanded Bellièvre to accede to the wishes of the Queen and her favorite.

Examples of Henry IV's often highhanded interference in judicial affairs could be multiplied. The few cases described above are sufficient to demonstrate that the King fully exercised his sovereign powers in matters of justice. However arbitrary his actions, Henry only followed in that tradition of the French monarchy which closely identified judicial power with the crown. As Roger Doucet has noted, the tradition of Saint-Louis, rendering his personal justice to his subjects, was still alive in the sixteenth century, if in greatly attenuated form.[16] The King's employment of his *justice retenue* and his use of extraordinary royal commissions did, nevertheless, evoke the protestations of the jurists. It is within the context of this protest that certain of Bellièvre's acts of resistance to royal decrees must be placed.

The opposition of the Chancellor, which was expressed by his refusal to seal letters and edicts of the crown, had a sound basis in the royal ordinances. Among the provisions of the Edict of Blois of 1579 was the following article defining the duties of the *garde des sceaux:* [17]

> Our *garde des sceaux* will seal three times weekly, on which days two or three *maîtres des requêtes* will be present . . . one of whom will sign the letters: they are warned to sign none contrary to the law or to our ordinances, on pain of answering for this in their own name.

15. *Ibid.*, pp. 301–2.
16. Doucet, *Institutions*, I, 89, 90.
17. *Recueil général des anciennes lois françaises, depuis l'an 420 jusqu'à la révolution de 1789,* ed. M. Isambert (Paris, 1829), XIV, 404.

More explicit still was a section of the oath of office taken by the chancellor, Antoine Duprat, in 1517: [18]

> When some letter signed at the command of the King is brought to you for sealing, if it is not just or reasonable, do not seal it until the aforesaid Lord commands it once or twice; but go before him and point out to him the reasons for which the letter is not reasonable. . . . If, after having heard the said reasons, he commands you to seal it, you will seal it because then the transgression will be the aforesaid Lord's and not yours.

The determination of the justness or reasonableness of royal acts allowed the chancellor to impose rather limited restraints upon the arbitrary conduct of the crown. Although such protests were usually futile, control of the seals provided the chancellor with the opportunity to serve as the conscience of the *robe longue* and, indeed, as the conscience of the king.

Possession of the seals of state allowed Bellièvre to delay the speedy execution of royal decrees. Thus, in matters which particularly distressed him, such as the practice of remitting penalties, he frequently utilized the limited check upon the monarchy's actions which his constitutional position permitted. The nature of the tactics followed by the Chancellor in such cases is well illustrated by the following letter of protest from the Duke of Sully: [19]

> At Rouen I spoke to you about an abolition which I desired to obtain from the King for a gentleman, nephew of Sieur de la Chevalerie. . . . His majesty having granted it, I begged you again at Caen to seal it. I again make the same supplication and if you wish to oblige me . . . it is time to put your hand to it.

Bellièvre justified his resistance in these instances by arguing that the King, like his subjects, should respect the law. In a letter to Henry IV, written in 1600, he opposed the annulling of a judgment against a murderer and warned that the King was in danger of undermining the very foundations of royal power by abolishing judicial sentences. The crown's subjects, Bellièvre explained, would love the King less if he retained in office men who did not perform their duties honestly. Duty

18. Quoted in *Lettres missives,* V, 665.
19. B.N., Ms. fr. 15897, fol. 520, Sully to Bellièvre, 25 September 1603.

required that the Chancellor admonish his master, "If abolitions are accorded, the door to the most outrageous wickedness is open." [20]

In his attempts to restore judicial authority and to impose restraints upon actions which he regarded as arbitrary or harmful, Bellièvre proved to be a most tenacious defender of proper legal procedures. When the King sought to exculpate the Viscount Neufvillette, who had killed a former member of the League, the Chancellor withheld the seals from the letters of abrogation for over three months. [21] The King was forced not only to issue several express commandments but also to send Sillery to Paris to present the royal arguments. While there is little evidence to suggest that Bellièvre's remonstrances changed Henry's will in these affairs, on occasion the Chancellor did obtain certain modifications of the King's letters and decrees. [22]

Bellièvre's resistance to improper procedures was not limited to the question of remitting penalties. The institution of an extraordinary royal commission to investigate the corrupt practices of minor local officials in Paris encountered the opposition of the Chancellor. [23] In another case, he refused to seal a royal edict providing for an inquiry into usury, contending that the edict conformed neither to the ordinances of the kingdom nor to the decrees of the parlement. [24] Royal grants of special privileges and letters creating new offices and nobles also came under the Chancellor's scrutiny. For example, in 1602 he protested the naming of a lieutenant general in the *baillage* of Rouen and Caen, claiming that "there will be similar demands for a lieutenancy in each province." [25] Likewise, his withholding the seals from patents of nobility bestowed by the crown was among the most common sources of friction between Bellièvre and the King. [26] The Chancellor also delayed the granting of public monies to specially favored individuals or interest groups. Several commandments from the King were required to force the Chancellor to seal a decree authorizing the transfer of tax revenues to a group of domestic manufac-

20. B.N., Ms. fr. 15894, fol. 377, Bellièvre to Henry IV, 1600.
21. *Lettres missives*, IX, 59, 78, 80.
22. *Ibid.*, p. 38; *Lettres inédites, 1603*, p. 55.
23. *Lettres missives*, IX, 21.
24. *Ibid.*, pp. 34–35, 51.
25. B.N., Ms. fr. 15894, fol. 443, Bellièvre to Henry IV, 6 April 1602.
26. *Lettres missives*, VI, 487; IX, 58, 79.

turers.[27] Another example of Bellièvre's concern for the financial integrity of the state was his refusal to seal letters endowing the Count of Soissons with the income from a tax on cloth.[28] Even the King's wishes in regard to his mistress, the Marquise of Verneuil, were on occasion impeded by the Chancellor. In 1602 Bellièvre antagonized Henry IV when he mounted a prolonged resistance, on legal grounds, to the legitimization of a royal bastard, the son of the Marquise.[29] At another time, both the King and the Duke of Sully had to intervene with the Chancellor to obtain the expedition of a monetary grant to the royal favorite.[30]

This pattern of obstructionism which characterized his tenure as chancellor provides an insight into Bellièvre's political role in the government of Henry IV. The Chancellor's stubborn legalism reflected his desire to maintain a balance between the crown and the constituted bodies. Although the religious wars had impressed upon him the necessity of a strong monarchy, Bellièvre looked with disfavor upon the erosion of the powers of judicial institutions, which was one of the consequences of absolutism. He was also opposed to the financial expedients of Sully and to the unnecessary expenditures of the King.[31] The proliferation of offices, as will be seen, was of particular concern to the Chancellor, and his opposition to the institutionalizing of venality embroiled him in a bitter dispute with Sully. An apologist for absolutism, Bellièvre was yet uneasy when confronted by the fact of absolute power. An officer who had battened upon the court, he recognized the dangers of that parasitism which sapped the financial resources of the state and country. His politics, then, were of a negative and restraining sort, designed to temper absolutism by the law and to serve the interests of the *robe longue.*

As the pre-eminent representative of the *robe longue* at the court of Henry IV, Bellièvre confronted a difficult problem of dual loyalties in his relations with the parlements. To the president of the Parlement of

27. *Ibid.,* IX, 48, 50.
28. *Ibid.,* V, 364.
29. B.N., Ms. fr. 15894, fol. 549, Bellièvre to Villeroy, 11 December 1602.
30. *Lettres missives,* IX, 82; B.N., Ms. fr. 15897, fol. 526, Sully to Bellièvre, 1603.
31. On this point, see Roland Mousnier, "Sully et Le Conseil d'état et des finances: la lutte entre Bellièvre et Sully," *Revue historique,* CXLII (1941), 83–84.

Toulouse the Chancellor once wrote, "My duty is to conserve the authority of the magistrates." [32] On numerous occasions, however, it fell to him, as the principal agent of the King in matters of justice, to impose the royal will upon recalcitrant parlements. To protect the dignity and interests of the sovereign courts, the Chancellor did in certain cases have recourse to the largely symbolic act of withholding the seals. Beyond this, all he could do was to attempt to convince the King to deal gently with the courts and to compromise the disputes which frequently erupted between the crown and the judicial bodies.

Illustrative of Bellièvre's attempts to preserve the authority of the magistrates was his intervention with the King in 1603 on behalf of the Parlement of Normandy. Friction between Henry IV and the sovereign court had arisen when the King granted an *évocation* removing all cases involving a Norman nobleman from the jurisdiction of the parlement. Henry summoned Bellièvre to the Louvre and commanded him to seal the *évocation*. "I said to the King," wrote the Chancellor, "that in my conscience I judged that it was not in the service of His Majesty to allow that the principal officers of justice in his province of Normandy should be so degraded of honor." [33] Those who had grievances against the nobleman, he pleaded, should not be denied their court of appeal. "It is a thing of dangerous consequence," he wrote, "that a gentleman who has power has no judge in the province where he lives." Following Bellièvre's appeal, the King agreed to strike certain abusive clauses from the edict of *évocation*. Henry persisted in his demand that the document be sealed, however, and the Chancellor, having discharged his constitutional obligations, reluctantly obeyed.

In the same year, a conflict developed between the crown and the Parlement of Brittany. The source of this disagreement was the sovereign court's refusal to receive as attorney general the royal appointee Jean Lefèvre. [34] The affair was resolved within the *Conseil d'état* by a select committee of *robins,* including Guillaume L'Aubespine and President de Calignon, over which the Chancellor presided. In his report to Henry IV, Bellièvre, acting upon the advice of his committee, urged that no punitive

32. B.N., Ms. fr. 15894, fol. 444, Bellièvre to Verdun, 24 September 1602.
33. *Ibid.,* fol. 577, Bellièvre to [?], 6 October 1603.
34. *Lettres inédites,* 1603, p. 63.

action be taken against the parlement. Condemnation of the court, he warned, would diminish the prestige of the magistrates among the people of Brittany and lead to disorders in that province.[35] The King accepted the advice of his Chancellor on condition that "the edict be prepared and sent to my parlement, and that it be followed and observed point by point."[36] Bellièvre then wrote the presidents of the sovereign court to inform the magistrates that their case had been handled by the "principal officers of the King who are of the *robe longue*" and to demand compliance with the royal edict.[37]

As mediator between the parlements and the crown, Bellièvre was able to secure from the King limited concessions and to preserve the sovereign courts from certain punitive actions. However minor these achievements, Bellièvre established himself during the years of his chancellorship as the outstanding defender of the law and a resourceful advocate of the interests of the legal order. Looking back upon the golden age of Henry IV, a *frondeur* would later place Bellièvre among those magistrates "whose statues should be erected in the most eminent place of the Grand Chambre of the Parlement."[38]

The appeals to the sanctity of the law, the reprimands to the King, and the frequent attempts to uphold the rights and dignity of the magistrates comprise the most interesting aspect of Bellièvre's chancellorship, for they illuminate one part of that ongoing struggle by the guardians of the law to contain absolutism within a constitutional framework. Bellièvre utilized that small margin of influence which he enjoyed in preference to most of the King's advisers, as well as the powers of his office, to shape or blunt royal policies and edicts in the higher interests of the well-ordered state as he conceived it. His constitutional role, however, should not obscure the obvious fact that Bellièvre was above all a crown servant, exercising the King's delegated authority, and a central figure in the royal bureaucracy. If in theory, and sometimes in practice, he represented the higher interests of the state, Bellièvre was the King's man whose duty it

35. B.N., Ms. fr. 15894, fol. 569, Bellièvre to Henry IV, 12 July 1603.

36. *Lettres inédites, 1603,* p. 64.

37. B.N., Ms. fr. 15894, fol. 571, Bellièvre to the Parlement of Brittany, July 1603.

38. *Choix de mazarinades,* ed. C. Moreau (Paris, 1853), I, 444.

was to maintain royal authority. Despite the obstructive tactics by which he sought to restrain Henry IV, the Chancellor remained, as always, the obedient and compliant creature of the crown.

III

IN HIS LETTERS PATENT endowing Bellièvre with the chancellorship, Henry IV had declared that a person of great probity and authority was needed to guarantee the protection of royal justice and finances.[39] The authority of the Chancellor was obviously limited. It would appear from his correspondence with Bellièvre, however, that the King relied upon the Chancellor's advice and allowed him wide latitude in the formulation and implementation of royal policies in matters concerning the administration of justice. For example, Henry wrote to Bellièvre on one occasion, I am grateful to you for having rejected the edicts proposed by the Baron of Solignac, since you judged them prejudicial to my service for the reasons you have written to me." [40] Another letter commanded the Chancellor to investigate a complaint of the crown's Protestant subjects and to "promptly remedy and order this as you judge necessary according to the intention of my edict." [41] Concerning a dispute among foreign workers in Paris, the King ordered Bellièvre to assemble the royal officials who had jurisdiction in the case "to see and consider what is most useful for the public and to order and enforce what is to be done in this." [42] These and numerous other letters of similar content confirm that in routine matters of justice and administration, when neither favoritism nor the personal interests of the crown were involved, Bellièvre exercised considerable discretionary powers in carrying out the King's business. Such administrative routine comprised the bulk of the Chancellor's duties, the nature of which remain to be examined.

The multifarious functions of the chancellorship allowed Bellièvre to enter into all aspects of judicial administration. He was, first of all, the principal representative of the crown in all cases which related to the

39. Duchesne, *Histoire des chanceliers*, p. 688.
40. *Lettres inédites, 1603*, p. 21.
41. *Lettres inédites, 1604*, p. 14.
42. *Lettres inédites, 1603*, p. 28.

security of the state and often took a direct hand in such affairs. The most notable of these was the treason trial of Marshal Biron, which occurred in 1602. Although all of the major councillors participated in the pretrial proceedings, it was Bellièvre who oversaw the conduct of Biron's trial and interrogated his accomplices.[43] In July 1602 the Chancellor assembled with the magistrates of the Parlement of Paris in the extraordinary session of the sovereign court which convicted Biron of treason. Following the conviction, Bellièvre degraded the traitor and pronounced the death penalty. In other less important police affairs, the Chancellor selected the judges, interrogated witnesses, and directed the work of the crown attorneys.

The primary function of the Chancellor was the supervision of the vast system of judicial administration. He served as the principal link, or at times as the buffer, between the sovereign power and the numerous administrative bodies in Paris and the provinces. On at least one occasion, in September 1600, Bellièvre acted directly in the ordering of the judicial system when he journeyed to Chambéry at the behest of the King. After conquering the city in August, Henry IV had written the Chancellor deploring the state of financial and judicial administration there. "Your presence," he wrote Bellièvre, "would bring order to everything." [44] The Chancellor immediately went to Savoy where he arranged for the appointment of a superintendent of justice and for the introduction of members of the Parlement of Grenoble into the high court of Chambéry. Overwhelmed by the demands for offices in the newly formed royal institutions, the Chancellor prepared for the King a roll of those whom he considered capable of serving in the bureaucracy and courts.[45]

Such excursions into the field were rare for the aging Chancellor, who normally superintended the work of the royal officials from Paris. At the very center of the bureaucracy, Bellièvre directed the activities of provincial officers, *commissaires,* and extraordinary royal commissions. When, in 1603, Henry dispatched a special agent to discipline the Parlement of

43. *Lettres inédites du Roi Henri IV au Chancelier Bellièvre, 1602,* ed. E. Halphen (Paris, 1883), pp. 21, 26; B.N., Ms. fr. 15894, fols. 530–33, Bellièvre to Henry IV, 11 July 1602.

44. *Lettres inédites,* p. 303.

45. B.N., Ms. fr. 15894, fols. 370–72ᵛ, Bellièvre to Henry IV, September 1600.

Normandy, he wrote Bellièvre, "You will instruct him well and long, particularly on what he must do and say there for my service."[46] Among the Chancellor's papers are numerous communications from field administrators and local officials which indicate that his involvement in administrative affairs extended to the lowest levels of jurisdiction. The crown's attorneys and officers in the *sénéchaussées* and *présidials* looked to the chancery for the clarification of royal edicts and repeatedly sought Bellièvre's recommendations on cases before them. Field administrators reported directly to the Chancellor, who provided them with their commissions and with other documents necessary for their investigations.

Provincial officials also had recourse to the Chancellor for the redress of grievances. Disputes among officers regarding jurisdictional rights or matters of protocol were often referred to him for resolution. From urban magistrates, Bellièvre received complaints against the royal officials who subverted the rights and privileges of the cities. Appeals from minor officials against abuses of justice by more highly placed officers were directed to the Chancellor, who was responsible for good order in the judicial system. An example of such an appeal was the protest of a *prévôt* of Turenne against the lieutenant general of Bourbonnais, who was accused of removing the cases of certain murderers and forgers from the jurisdiction of the *prévôté,* and against the King, who had remitted the death penalty imposed upon a local nobleman. Bellièvre intervened with the King on behalf of the *prévôt,* arguing that if justice were so perverted, "You will cause a good officer to lose heart."[47] As in other cases in which Bellièvre attempted to uphold the cause of the lower courts against the appeals of the King's friends, this intervention proved fruitless.[48] Thus, the Chancellor was the principal mediator, although not the ultimate judge, among the many competing agencies of the kingdom's government.

Although Henry IV actively participated in all aspects of administration, he normally relied upon the Chancellor to represent the royal will to the judicial bodies. All *évocations* and remissions of penalties passed through Bellièvre's hands. He not only sealed such decrees but also

46. *Lettres inédites, 1604,* p. 14.
47. B.N., Ms. fr. 15894, fol. 467, Bellièvre to Henry IV, June 1603.
48. *Lettres inédites, 1603,* p. 51.

oversaw their implementation. In certain cases, it was the Chancellor's function to assign cognizance to particular judges or courts. Aside from this administrative routine, Bellièvre frequently entered into the judicial process directly at the behest of the King. On one occasion, Henry commanded him to intervene with the *présidial* of Tours to obtain exemplary punishment for a band of robbers who had stolen arms from the royal chateau of Vendôme.[49] In another letter to Bellièvre, the King complained that the delays in the trial of an officer of the Parlement of Dauphiné set a bad example, and he ordered the Chancellor to see that the case was judged quickly and according to its merits.[50] More often, as has been noted, Henry instructed Bellièvre to intervene with a court not to serve justice but rather to preserve a royal client from the judgment of the magistrates.

Of highest importance in the administration of justice were the relations between the crown and the sovereign courts. Although an advocate of the interests of the parlements, Bellièvre was responsible for the maintenance of royal authority, and, consequently, it was his first duty to impose discipline upon the courts. In August 1600 Henry twice ordered Bellièvre to secure from the Parlement of Toulouse the verification of an edict creating new offices in the lower courts of Languedoc. "I know they will believe what you command them," the King wrote, "and I ask you to dispatch a letter in my name by which you will make known my dissatisfaction with them."[51] When the Parlement of Normandy refused to verify an edict, Henry commanded the Chancellor to summon the president of the court and demand obedience. "If they force me to use extreme measures," he warned Bellièvre, "they will regret having so little regard for my commandments. Speak to the president in this manner and add whatever you judge to be appropriate."[52] Again, in 1603, when the Parlement of Normandy was accused of extending its investigatory powers beyond the terms of a royal edict, the Chancellor was instructed to look into the matter and, if necessary, revoke the edict.[53]

49. *Lettres missives,* IX, 104–5.
50. *Ibid.,* pp. 86–87.
51. *Ibid.,* V, 273.
52. *Ibid.,* p. 426.
53. *Lettres inédites, 1603,* p. 53.

As administrator and protector of the King's justice, Bellièvre was clearly less a servant of the state than an agent of the monarchy who echoed the voice of his master to the parlements and other judicial institutions. He was no mere lackey, however, and the powers inherent in his office did give him some control over the kingdom's affairs. Although the government of Henry IV was less complex than the bureaucratic machine of the later seventeenth century, the King was, nonetheless, dependent upon his high administrators and councillors for information and advice. Because of Bellièvre's expert knowledge of the workings of the government, his connections in the provinces, and his commanding position in the royal bureaucracy, Henry naturally turned to him for recommendations on the conduct of internal affairs. As has been noted, the King granted the Chancellor discretionary powers in the administration of justice. In addition, control of the seals provided Bellièvre with a means of influencing policy in minor ways and of asserting his political views. The Chancellor also enjoyed the power of patronage. Many royal appointments and grants of privileges passed through his hands, and this allowed him to exercise some influence upon the recruitment of the King's officers.

Ultimately, however, the real power of any high office derived not from its attributes per se but from the influence which the holder exerted upon the sovereign. In Bellièvre's case, administrative power was less important than the political power which belonged to him by virtue of his position as president of the council. It was, after all, in the royal councils, and not in the chancery, that the important decisions were made. The *Conseil d'état,* in the early years of the seventeenth century, was the scene of a dramatic confrontation between the aging Bellièvre and the rising figure at court, the Duke of Sully. At stake in this clash was the favor of the King, the most important form of power for crown servants in the absolutist state.

IV

ASIDE FROM THE SUPERVISION of judicial affairs, the Chancellor presided over the royal councils in the absence of the King. This function was potentially the most important attributed to his office, for it involved Bellièvre in all the major business of the central government, both domestic and foreign. As president of the council, Bellièvre received the royal directives ordering particular actions upon the councillors, and through him the recommendations of the King's principal advisers were dispatched to the perambulating court. Likewise, all edicts emanating from the *Conseil d'état* bore his signature. The routine forms by which the King's business was ordered and expedited, however, indicate little or nothing about the actual distribution of power within the government. Until his death in 1607, Bellièvre continued to perform the formal duties of the chancellorship. Yet power and influence had long since passed from his hands into those of younger and more vigorous men.

The years of Bellièvre's chancellorship coincided roughly with Sully's rise from chief financial officer of the crown to a commanding position in the councils of Henry IV.[54] His ascendancy led to a significant weakening of the collegial principle of administration at the highest level and to the gradual displacement of Bellièvre as the first councillor of the King. When he took up his functions as chancellor in the late summer of 1599, Bellièvre was at the height of his powers and his fame. His long experience in government, his tenure as intendant in Lyons, and above all his part in negotiating the peace with Spain assured him a favorable hearing at court and an important role as adviser to the crown. Of the men to whom Henry entrusted his most weighty affairs, none had more prestige than the Chancellor. By the beginning of 1605, however, Sully was the effective leader of the *Conseil d'état,* and Sillery had replaced the Chancellor as *garde des sceaux.* The story of Bellièvre's decline from power allows us to focus not only upon an important incident in the court politics of the time but also, and of greater importance, upon the changes in the structure of government which marked the second half of Henry IV's reign.

At the heart of that government, of course, stood the King. No one who has perused the administrative documents of the period can doubt that Henry IV was King in fact. The principal advisers of the crown, including Sully (who tended greatly to exaggerate his influence upon policy making), were servants of the King and not manipulators of the royal will. Henry did, nevertheless, delegate considerable authority to his most intimate councillors and relied upon them for advice. Although an

54. Mousnier, "Sully et Le Conseil," p. 80.

absolutist in his conception of his princely office, the King was no despot. Following in the tradition of the French monarchy, he ruled with the aid of his councillors but allowed neither the *Conseil d'état* nor the collective decisions of the *Conseil d'affaires* to limit his actions in any significant way.[55]

For approximately a decade after the conclusion of the struggle with the Duke of Mayenne, the tasks of advising the King on matters of state were shared by Bellièvre, Villeroy, Sully, Sillery, Jeannin, and a handful of other councillors. The official documents of the reign reveal little about the actual workings of the government, but from the administrative correspondence which passed between the court and the Chancellor, certain conclusions may be drawn about the decision-making process.

First, the important business of raising issues before the crown and offering recommendations was a collective effort; differences among the principal advisers were resolved by the will of the King. In 1603, for example, Bellièvre and Sillery, both experienced in Swiss affairs, urged Henry to make good his financial obligations to the cantons. "I have shown the letter which you sent me . . . to M. de Villeroy and President Jeannin," Sillery wrote Bellièvre, "and following their advice I informed the King of its contents. And on this occasion, I particularly emphasized the state of Swiss affairs to make him aware of the harm along with the remedies."[56] Later, Sillery assured the Chancellor that the King recognized the importance of the Swiss problem and would soon arrange for the necessary payments. In what was perhaps a reference to Sully, he wrote Bellièvre, "Your voice and your authority must have enlightened and taught those who have no knowledge in these affairs."[57] The Chancellor's objections to a project designed to promote the immigration of foreign artisans and merchants into France met with a different response, as the following dispatch from Sillery suggests:[58]

I represented to His Majesty, in the presence of Monsieur de Rosny and Monsieur de Villeroy, the considerations which had been set forth

55. Doucet, *Institutions,* I, 144.
56. B.N., Ms. fr. 15899, fol. 109, Sillery to Bellièvre, 5 March 1603.
57. *Ibid.,* fol. 110, Sillery to Bellièvre, March 1603.
58. *Ibid.,* fol. 122, Sillery to Bellièvre, 18 September 1603. The Rosny referred to in this letter is, of course, Sully.

by the gentlemen of the council. The King persisted in his will to introduce foreigners into France and ordered me to consult with M. de Rosny . . . and to draw up a declaration which will be sent to you by M. de Rosny.

Generally, then, the King acted, in both domestic and foreign affairs, only after consultations with the members of the councils. In 1600, when Henry considered promoting his own candidacy for the vacant office of Holy Roman Emperor, it was to Bellièvre, Villeroy, and Sully that he turned for advice.[59] On another occasion, the King wrote to Bellièvre, "I have not wanted to declare my will to the Sieur Dauphin, deputy of the city of Geneva, without having the advice of my council." [60] Henry then commanded the Chancellor, Sully, Jeannin, and Sillery to assemble and to consider the requests of the Swiss city. In matters of internal policy, Henry also relied, up to a point, on the recommendations of the collegiate advisory body. Regarding the expedition of financial edicts in May 1600, he wrote the Chancellor, "I understand that you will gather at your home tomorrow in a special council, and that you will arrive at some decision, my presence serving only to approve your resolutions, because if you expect some advice on this from me, I cannot give it." [61] Or again, when a royal *commissaire* in Poitou sent Bellièvre a report on the affairs of that province and on the complaints of the local nobility against the financial exactions of the crown, the Chancellor consulted with Villeroy and Sully and then advised the King on the action to be taken.[62] These, and other similar cases, suggest something of the manner in which the King's business was carried out but tell us little of the distribution of power among the high officers of state.

There is no evidence to suggest that, at the beginning of their association, any of the leading crown servants of Henry IV exercised a preponderant influence at court. Villeroy, who remained close to his perambulating master, conducted the King's correspondence and supervised the foreign affairs of the kingdom. Initially, at least, Sully and Bellièvre jointly oversaw the administration of internal affairs, and, of the two, the

59. J. Nouaillac, *Villeroy, secrétaire d'état et ministre de Charles IX, Henri III et Henri IV* (Paris, 1909), pp. 481–82.
60. *Lettres inédites, 1604*, p. 8.
61. *Lettres missives*, VIII, 766.
62. B.N., Fonds Dupuy 194, fol. 94, Bellièvre to Henry IV, 22 June 1601.

Chancellor undoubtedly possessed a higher authority.[63] The nature of the collaboration between the two great rivals is revealed in the administrative records of the period. Concerning the establishment of financial and judicial offices in Bresse, the King wrote Bellièvre in August 1600, "I shall leave this entirely to what you and Rosny shall advise, you for justice and he for finances." [64] The differentiation of functions, however, was not as clearly defined as the preceding example might indicate. Because the *Conseil d'état* was very much involved in fiscal questions, Bellièvre, as presiding officer, was inevitably drawn into financial affairs. Thus, the Chancellor and Sully often worked together on problems of fiscal administration.[65] Evidence of their collaboration is to be found in a letter, written to the King by Bellièvre in 1602, in which the Chancellor reported that he and Sully had conferred and agreed that a proposed plan to alienate portions of the royal domain was detrimental to the interests of the crown.[66] In November 1602 Sully informed the Chancellor, "The first business I thought of, having arrived here, was to expedite, in the form which we decided upon in the council, the declaration which must be sent to the *Cour des aides* . . . which I have adjusted according to your advice." [67] At another time, Sully wrote Bellièvre regarding two commandments issued to the financial officers, "I have expedited two declarations such as I judged appropriate; all, nonetheless, submitted to your judgment and correction." [68] Thus, the little evidence bearing directly on the early relationship between chancellor and councillor suggests that Sully, at most, enjoyed an equality of functions.

V

THE BALANCE OF POWER within the circle of intimate advisers of Henry IV was soon disrupted, however, by the rise of Sully to a dominant position. A clash between the councillor and the aging Chancellor be-

63. This point has also been made by Roland Mousnier in "Sully et Le Conseil," p. 80.
64. *Lettres inédites,* p. 256.
65. B.N., Ms. fr. 15894, fols. 327, 365–66.
66. B.N., Ms. fr. 15577, fol. 273, Bellièvre to Henry IV, 20 August 1602.
67. B.N., Ms. fr. 15897, fol. 521, Sully to Bellièvre, 10 November 1602.
68. *Ibid.,* fol. 519, Sully to Bellièvre, 13 October 1599.

came inevitable as the power and the ambitions of the royal favorite increased. The animosity between these two crown servants was deep-rooted and marked both by a petty conflict of personalities and by serious differences over major issues. The Duke of Sully had only contempt for Bellièvre and his kind. An incident which occurred in 1600 perhaps best revealed his scornful attitude toward the *robins* at court. In that year, war with Savoy threatened, and among the royal councillors opinion was divided as to the advisability of undertaking a campaign. Sully was, of course, a warhawk, while Bellièvre quite naturally opposed an action which promised to undermine the peace established in 1598. In his memoirs, Sully recorded that the Chancellor approached him urging temporization. "We have so happily worked at the Peace of Vervins," Bellièvre reportedly said, "and you are going to overturn all that we have done." Sully claimed to have made the following reply: [69]

> Ho! Ho! Monsieur, you take alarm quickly. That is pardonable in those of your robe; but when I discuss this with the King and the good captains I shall make them see that Monsieur de Savoy has founded his principal defense on the timidity of those who resemble you and on the fine promises of others who, thinking to deceive the King, will ruin the Duke of Savoy.

In this particular instance Sully won out, and the war was undertaken. However much embellished in the writing, this incident indicates the great differences of character between Bellièvre, cautious and peace-loving, and Sully, ever bold, bellicose, and extremely conscious of his personal power.

The conflict of the two men, as it descended into personal pettiness, was not without its amusing side. When, in 1603, Sully was appointed *grand voyer*, Bellièvre withheld the seals from the royal letters patent endowing his rival with the rights and privileges of the office. Sully, in turn, accused the Chancellor of treating him "like the least person in France who obtains some favor from the King." "For almost two months," he wrote Bellièvre, "you have had in your hands two declarations of the King concerning my charge of *grand voyer*. . . . It seems to

---

69. Sully, "Mémoires des sages et royales oeconomies d'estat de Henri Le Grand," *Nouvelle Collection des mémoires relatifs à l'histoire de France,* ed. M. Michaud (Paris, 1881), XVII, p. 330.

me that I should not be dealt with in this manner. . . . I have such shame that I dare not speak to anyone." [70] Thus did the Chancellor avenge the many humiliations which he suffered at Sully's hands.

The arena in which the struggle between the two crown servants took place was the royal council. Through the Chancellor's correspondence with his old friend Villeroy, the development of this bitter feud may be followed. In December 1602, a crisis erupted when Bellièvre delayed acting upon certain financial measures which had been proposed by Sully in the *Conseil d'état.* Of Sully's conduct in this affair, the Chancellor wrote the following to Villeroy: [71]

> He demanded that I explain myself as if I were a clerk of finances. I have borne all up to the present, while seeing that he seeks to make himself master of the council. I have resolved to protest to the King with all humility that it is not reasonable that so young a man as he, who is only beginning to understand the world, should undertake to teach me a lesson. You know by the letter which I have written to the King that I feel too scorned. That does not cause me to lose courage . . . but being treated as I am, I have no authority to do what I otherwise could for the service of the King.

Bellièvre's outburst was inspired by a letter from the King in which Henry, acting upon Sully's advice, reprimanded the Chancellor for his procrastination in dealing with financial affairs. "I have wanted to write you this," the King stated, "to tell you, following my commandment, to work in all diligence . . . so that I recognize that you are as devoted to what is of my service as to what is of your own particular interest." [72] This letter, which called into question both his efficiency and his integrity, forced Bellièvre to defend himself from Sully's accusations. In a long communication to Henry IV, the Chancellor claimed that he had carried out the King's instructions in the presence of Sully.[73] For the inactivity of the *Conseil d'état,* he blamed the intendants of finance. In eight days, Bellièvre told the King, he handled more business than the intendants did in eight months. Regarding his own performance, he wrote, "I do not see that your subjects complain that I do not fairly render justice to them, nor, as

70. B.N., Ms. fr. 15897, fol. 522, Sully to Bellièvre, 1603.
71. B.N., Ms. fr. 15894, fol. 547, Bellièvre to Villeroy, December 1602.
72. *Lettres missives,* IX, 26.
73. B.N., Ms. fr. 15894, fol. 437, Bellièvre to Henry IV, December 1602.

sick as I have been, that the affairs of Your Majesty are retarded." Against the charge of self-interest, Bellièvre contended, "I have no plan to aggrandize my house . . . being able to say that since I entered Your Majesty's service I have not increased my wealth by one hundred *sous* of rentes." In the same month, he complained to Villeroy that Sully had delayed in providing funds for a special *commissaire* to be sent to Brittany. "This refusal," he warned the Secretary, "forces me to neglect the service of the King." [74]

Bellièvre and Sully clashed again over the administration of finances in May 1603. To Villeroy, the Chancellor protested that Sully treated him like a *chauffe-cire*.[75] Objecting to the highhanded methods of the finance minister, Bellièvre wrote, "This new president of the council will presume to force me to pass upon affairs at his will." In the *Conseil d'état*, he informed Villeroy, "He [Sully] demanded why I had not sealed this edict, and he spoke of his power more than he ever had. . . . I can no longer support such offenses." At issue in this controversy was a question of proper procedures. Sully sought to expedite a tax edict over the objections of the *Chambre des comptes,* while the Chancellor insisted that the forms of administration should be maintained. When Sully sent two of his men to hector Bellièvre, the latter replied "that I would meet in the council with him, and that I would facilitate that which is the King's will." [76] It was, then, Sully's assertion of his personal power, outside of the normal administrative processes, which the Chancellor resisted.

The struggle between Bellièvre and Sully involved a conflict both of personalities and of generations. Of greater importance, however, was the fact that fundamental differences of opinion on matters of state policy divided the two crown servants. In foreign affairs, as we have seen, Bellièvre utilized his influence to maintain the precarious peace achieved at Vervins and to encourage an unadventurous foreign policy. "In matters of state," he once wrote regarding relations with Spain, "we have a maxim that we must not create tensions where it is not necessary." [77] Sully, on the

---

74. B.N., Ms. fr. 15577, fol. 325, Bellièvre to Villeroy, December 1602.
75. B.N., Ms. fr. 15894, fol. 562, Bellièvre to Villeroy, 28 May 1603. A *chauffe-cire* was a minor chancery official.
76. *Ibid.*
77. *Ibid.,* fol. 582.

other hand, advocated a more active and belligerent policy. When Henry briefly considered entering the competition for the imperial crown, Bellièvre opposed the move, and Sully warmly supported it.[78] The under-cover war with Spain, which was begun after the signing of the treaty at Vervins, found support among those, like Sully, who desired an open break between the two states. An undated memorandum written by Bellièvre, probably in 1603 or 1604, reveals that Sully on one occasion sought to commit Henry IV to an alliance with England and brought his proposal before the council.[79] Although the Chancellor accepted the necessity of covert aid to the Dutch in their struggle with Spain, he did not favor an open alliance with the English. Such a treaty, he argued, would lead to a war which would pose far more difficulties for France than for England. France, Bellièvre noted, was open to invasion on all sides, whereas England enjoyed a protected position. In such matters, the Chancellor warned, one should not trust Sully's judgment but, rather, turn to those "who think more deeply about this affair."

On questions of domestic policy, there were equally sharp differences of opinion between the two antagonists. For one thing, Sully desired to introduce a greater number of the nobility of the sword into the government of Henry IV.[80] Bellièvre, in turn, sought to surround the King with members of the *robe longue,* who would serve as a kind of permanent high bureaucracy. The Chancellor's thoughts on the administrative role of the *robe longue* were set forth in greatest detail in an undated memorandum, addressed to Henry IV, on the reform of the *Conseil du roi.*[81] When he entered the royal service after Henry II's death, Bellièvre noted, the King's council was dominated by a few experienced administrators such as Morvillier and Sébastien L'Aubespine. In the ensuing years, an increasing number of great lords, both secular and ecclesiastical, and high royal officials had gained entry into the various councils which composed the *Conseil du roi.* It was neither desirable nor possible, the Chancellor conceded, to deprive the kingdom's notables of their access to the royal council. However, to assure greater administrative efficiency, Bellièvre

78. Nouaillac, *Villeroy,* pp. 481–82.
79. B.N., Ms. fr. 15894, fols. 583–84, Bellièvre to [?], n.d.
80. On this point, see Mousnier, "Sully et Le Conseil," p. 82.
81. B.N., Ms. fr. 15894, fols. 438–39.

proposed that Henry appoint up to eight councillors of the *robe longue* to represent the crown in the *Conseil d'état* and in the *Conseil des parties* (which was largely concerned with matters of administrative justice). Of the eight, four were to remain close to the King during any given six-month period, and four were to be present in the councils. Among those suggested by Bellièvre to serve in this capacity were Sillery, Jeannin, Calignon, the intendant of finances, and two councillors, Maisse and Pontcarré. "I include here no ecclesiastical prelates or seigneurs following the military profession," the Chancellor wrote, "except the Archbishop of Bourges . . . and Monsieur de Rosny . . . who is obliged to be in the company of Your Majesty, because he bears primary responsibility for your finances." Of particular interest, in light of his feud with Sully, was the Chancellor's suggestion that a special council be created to deal with financial administration. Bellièvre's memorandum to the King had a twofold significance. In the first place, it indicated his determination to maintain in high positions of authority members of his own estate. Moreover, his plan for the reform of the royal council revealed a reasonably sophisticated understanding of the requirements of a rational administration, among which was a certain continuity in procedures and personnel at the highest levels.

Together with his desire to reform the administrative and advisory bodies, Bellièvre sought to restore the practice of the King governing in his council. His objections concerned Henry's increasing reliance upon Sully and the consequent aggrandizement of the finance minister's personal power, which lessened the importance of the councillors generally. The Chancellor's misgivings were expressed in the following letter to Villeroy: [82]

> I shall tell you also that when the council is separated from the King . . . ordinances are announced . . . which we send to the provinces, which are made by Monsieur de Rosny and the Chancellor, and he and I do not have the standing to send commandments in the kingdom.

In addition, the Chancellor complained that "When the king is not present in his council, he cannot give the contentment to his subjects which otherwise he might." Obviously, Bellièvre feared the rise of government by a prime minister, which would erode the powers of the royal

82. *Ibid.*, fol. 544, Bellièvre to Villeroy, November 1602.

council. By insisting that the King alone possessed the authority to give commandments to the kingdom, he implicitly denied Sully's right to exercise delegated authority in the King's name.

Aside from their disagreement over the administrative role of the *robe longue* and the place of the council in the King's government, Bellièvre and Sully held widely divergent views on questions of financial policy. The principal conflict between Bellièvre and his adversary centered on Sully's proposal to institutionalize the venality of offices by making the majority of positions in the royal service inheritable through the device of an annual payment. Although essentially a revenue measure, Sully's plan involved both political and social questions of great importance. The debate over the edict took place within the *Conseil d'état* and extended over a period of nearly two years. Bellièvre used every instrument at his command to delay and to modify a measure which he regarded as harmful to sound finances, justice, and social harmony in the kingdom.[83]

In November 1602 the Chancellor reported to Villeroy that Sully had presented an edict to the council by which "those who paid annually a sixtieth part of the value of their offices . . . would be allowed to resign them to whomever they pleased." [84] After a sharp debate, the measure passed the council, causing Bellièvre to remark, "As soon as one speaks of money, all reason ceases. May God have pity on this kingdom." The Chancellor based his opposition to the proposal on both political and economic grounds. The King, he warned, would be deprived of the right to select his own officers. "He would be constrained to receive as *président aux enquêtes,* who directs the young councillors, a fool, a corrupt man who would bring disorder to the chamber." Concerning his supervision of judicial appointments, he wrote, "I can no longer question him, if I judge him to be a wicked man. I can no longer reject him without allowing him a legal hearing." The crown's officials, Bellièvre continued, "will no longer be officers of the King, they will be officers of their purses."

The most harmful effect of Sully's project, Bellièvre maintained, would

83. For an excellent analysis of the debate over the *Paulette* and of its wider implications, the reader is referred to Roland Mousnier's article. Although the paragraphs which follow are based upon a reading of the original materials, the conclusions differ in no fundamental respect from those of Professor Mousnier.
84. B.N., Ms. fr. 15894, fols. 544–45, Bellièvre to Villeroy, November 1602.

be the proliferation of offices which it would stimulate. "By means of this edict," he wrote, "you will cause the provinces to lose hope of ever seeing the suppression of judicial and other officers from whom they suffer such great ruin. . . . We are at peace, and these novelties will teach the people that peace is harsher for them than war." The Chancellor concluded his letter to Villeroy on a note of despair: "There are infinite other inconveniences, but money speaks, and reason and honor are silent."

Despair, however, did not mean capitulation. Bellièvre refused to discontinue his opposition to the edict, despite the support given by a majority of the council to Sully's expedient plan, and he prepared a lengthy memorandum for the King outlining more completely the reasons for his disapproval.[85]

The principal argument advanced by the proponents of the so-called *Paulette* was that it would augment the annual revenues of the crown by some 400,000 *livres*. This was a particularly important consideration, because, as Bellièvre noted, the monarchy confronted the prospect of a deficit of 300,000 *livres* in 1603. Nevertheless, the Chancellor held that "The remedy is worse than the evil." The immediate economic advantages which the edict offered, he warned, were outweighed by the harm which it would do to the King's service. Into the royal judiciary would be attracted the most avaricious and corrupt men in the kingdom—profiteers who sought only their own gain. "Good laws are necessary," Bellièvre wrote, "but the laws are useless if there is not a good magistrate to exercise them." In addition, both the King and the parlements would be deprived of their respective rights of appointing and approving magistrates. As a result, the authority of the crown would be seriously limited, and all hope of reform within the sovereign courts would be lost.

Furthermore, Bellièvre objected that the *Paulette* was detrimental to the interests of the older, established families of the *robe longue*. If Henry approved the edict, the Chancellor warned, "Honest men . . . can no longer hope that for the service which they have rendered His Majesty, he will raise them to any office." This in turn would lead to a deterioration in

85. This memorandum is conveniently reproduced in "Contre La Paulette: mémoire du Chancelier Bellièvre," ed. Et. Fages, *Revue Henri IV*, I (1906), 182–88. The manuscript version (B.N., Ms. fr. 15894, fols. 450–54) contains notations by one of Bellièvre's secretaries.

the quality of service performed by the royal officials. Finally, Bellièvre protested that the older families would no longer be able to place their children in the courts:

> Offices will climb to such excessive and unreasonable prices that no gentleman will want or will be able to place his children in the sovereign courts. . . . Nor will the presidents or the councillors be able to place their children. They do not acquire the riches . . . by which their children may arrive at such an estate. We shall see in the parlement only the children of those whose fathers have not been of quality but who have managed their affairs well . . . from which will come a great scorn of, indeed corruption of, justice.

France, in the future, would be overrun by profiteering jurists who would do irreparable harm to the courts and to the country's economy. "There is nothing in this kingdom so hateful and damaging to the people," Bellièvre concluded in his appeal to the King, "as the multiplicity of offices, which is such that half of the *taille* is employed for their wages, commerce is abandoned, and many who could serve in the military, in agriculture, and in the arts . . . spend their lives exercising offices and serve only to devour and ruin the people." The essential reform, he argued, was to pare down the overgrown bureaucracy and court, which threatened to strangle all productivity and undermine the sound financing of the state.

The memorandum against the *Paulette* was the single most significant policy statement issued by Bellièvre. If Sully demonstrated a certain realism in accepting the fact of venality and seeking to profit from it, the Chancellor, by clearly and correctly pointing out the long-range implications of the edict, proved to be the higher realist and the sounder adviser of the King. With great clarity he condemned the fiscal expediency of the *Paulette* and rightly pointed out the dangers of that parasitism which would burden the state throughout the *ancien régime*. Bellièvre's views, however, reflected more than a high-minded concern for the well-being of the people, of the monarchy, and of the state. As the leading spokesman of the *robe longue,* the Chancellor stubbornly resisted a measure which appeared to undermine the hereditary power of the established officeholding families. Over the period of a century or more, such families as the Bellièvres had entrenched themselves in the royal judiciary through many of the practices which the Chancellor condemned. Indeed, the history of the Bellièvres in the sixteenth and seventeenth centuries provides an excellent case study of nepotism. Like any elite, the *robe longue* advanced an ethos and self-image to explain its favored place in society. To the Chancellor, the *robins* were honest, loyal, and devoted servants of the crown, trained for the judiciary, who fully deserved the rewards which hereditary officeholding brought. The newly rich, on the other hand, were outsiders with no tradition of service behind them and, of greatest interest, no claims to "quality." Thus, Bellièvre's argument joined sound political and economic reasons with the self-interested views of the legal order, which desired to close its ranks and to assure its control of the kingdom's judicial institutions by asserting the claims of birth.

In 1604, the *Paulette* was promulgated. Bellièvre's ideas, one of his secretaries recorded, "did not have as much influence on the mind of the King as the desire to increase his revenue." [86] For many months, however, the Chancellor resisted both Sully and the King, first by withholding his signature from the edict and then by his refusal to consider the project in the *Conseil d'état*.[87] Through such tactics, Bellièvre did secure several amendments to the original proposal of November 1602. Of greatest importance was the provision by which the King retained control of the offices of first president of Parlement, prosecuting attorney, and crown attorney. Among the provincial judicial offices, that of lieutenant general remained exempt from the rules set down in the *Paulette*. The Chancellor's ability to force upon Sully certain revisions of the edict indicates that, at least until 1604, he continued to exercise considerable authority within the government and to influence, or modify, royal policies. Above all, this episode demonstrates the remarkable skill with which Bellièvre exercised the powers of his office.

It was, nonetheless, during the period of the extended debate over the *Paulette* that the powers of the Chancellor began to wane. From 1602, when he first challenged Bellièvre's control of the *Conseil d'état*, Sully increasingly dominated the central administrative and advisory body. As early as December 1603, the ambassador of the Grand Duke of Tuscany

---

86. B.N., Ms. fr. 15894, fol. 452.
87. On Bellièvre's tactics in the council, see Mousnier, "Sully et Le Conseil," pp. 74, 76.

reported that an intrigue was under way at court designed to withdraw the state seals from the Chancellor.[88] Although Bellièvre retained all of the outward forms of power, he was, by 1605, merely a figurehead. A small incident which occurred in 1604 illustrates his declining influence. Concerning a minor affair involving the Duke of Lorraine, the King ordered Bellièvre to summon the principal councillors. At the same time, Henry wrote to Sully, "You will see to it that all things pass as they should." [89] Thus Sully, always the royal favorite among the councillors, had become the effective chief of the council.

VI

THE DOWNFALL OF BELLIÈVRE came at the very end of 1604 when his colleague Sillery was named *garde des sceaux*. Under letters verified by the Parlement of Paris in March 1605, Sillery was to "exercise in the absence of . . . the Chancellor . . . all functions which depend on him with the same power which the chancellors have customarily enjoyed." [90] In a letter to the Cardinal du Perron, Bellièvre wrote of the King's decision: [91]

> You have heard of the resolution concerning my affairs. . . . The King had me come to his *cabinet de gallerie* and told me in the presence of the Queen that it was his enemies who wanted to deprive me of the seals, that it was never his will, that I had served too well and should keep them all my life.

Sillery's function, Henry had explained, was to relieve the Chancellor of his duties when the latter was incapacitated by illness. To solidify the new relationship between Bellièvre and Sillery on a basis of friendship, the King suggested that a marriage alliance be arranged. Hence, Nicolas Bellièvre and Claude Brulart were betrothed by royal command.

Whatever the King's claims of loyalty to his aged Chancellor,

88. *Ibid.,* p. 80; *Négotiations diplomatiques de La France avec La Toscane,* ed. Abel Desjardins (Paris, 1886), V, 519.
89. *Lettres missives,* VI, 199–200.
90. B.N., Ms. fr., nouv. acq. 3359, fol. 317.
91. B.N., Fonds Dupuy 194, fol. 106, Bellièvre to Du Perron, 1 January 1605.

Bellièvre's powers from 1605 were nominal. In September of that year, Bassompierre recorded the following of a meeting which he had with Bellièvre at Artenay: [92]

> I saw in passing the chancellor . . . who, upon leaving Tours, had left the seals in the hands of the *garde des sceaux* de Sillery. I met him as he was walking in a garden. . . . He said to me: Monsieur, you see a man who is going to Paris to find a sepulcher. I have served the kings as much as I have been able, and when they have seen that I was no longer capable, they have sent me to repose and to prepare for the salvation of my soul, which their affairs have prevented me from thinking about.

When Bassompierre reminded the Chancellor that he still had the right to preside over the council, Bellièvre reportedly replied, "My friend, a chancellor without seals is an apothecary without sugar." Indeed, the loss of the seals represented a total decline of power and influence.

Bellièvre's fall from power cannot be attributed solely, or perhaps even chiefly, to the enmity of Sully. The Chancellor had incurred the displeasure of the King by supporting Marie de Medici during the period of Henry's romance with Henriette d'Entragues.[93] Finally, there can be little doubt that Bellièvre, at the age of seventy-five, had outlived his usefulness to the monarchy. In his journal, L'Estoile made no mention of the intrigues which surrounded the Chancellor's displacement, noting only that the King had discharged Bellièvre because of his age.[94] During the last two years of his life, the Chancellor continued to preside over the royal council and over the administrative routine of the chancery. As late as August 1607, only weeks before Bellièvre's death, we find Henry writing the chancellor concerning a petty affair of financial administration.[95] Important state business, however, was handled by Sully, Villeroy, Sillery, and the younger councillors. When, for example, the Chancellor assigned Sillery to judge a case involving the Bishop of Senlis and his

92. Maréchal de Bassompierre, *Mémoires du Maréchal de Bassompierre,* ed. M. de Chantérac (Paris, 1870), I, 171–72.
93. Mousnier, "Sully et Le Conseil," p. 85.
94. L'Estoile, *Journal,* II, 270.
95. *Lettres missives,* VII, 343.

canons, the King replied, "Sillery is now *garde des sceaux* and therefore occupied with other affairs of greater consequence." [96] With Bellièvre's death in September 1607, the chancellorship went to Sillery, who brought to the high office neither the distinction nor the integrity of his predecessor.

96. *Ibid.,* p. 206.

CHAPTER SIX

A Robe Dynasty

BELLIÈVRE'S FALL FROM POWER removed from court politics the most important figure in a long-lived dynasty of royal officials and magistrates. Once again, as in 1588, a single act of the sovereign's will reduced this loyal crown servant to political impotence. His high office had not protected Bellièvre from the ultimate humiliation which was so often the courtier's fate. The court, however, was not only the stage upon which careers were made and destroyed; it was also the center of that complex web of interests and patronage through which great families were nourished and sustained. Early in this study, the family factor was introduced to evoke the setting of court life as it involved the administrators and councillors of the *robe longue*. There remains, by way of conclusion, to pick up the threads of family history and to examine the later Bellièvres as a court dynasty.

From the middle decades of the fifteenth century, the status and power of the Bellièvres in French society had been achieved within the framework of the judicial, administrative, and ecclesiastical institutions of the

kingdom. Each stage in the family's rise had been marked by its association with a particular elite—urban, provincial-judicial, and, finally, high
administrative. With Pomponne de Bellièvre, the family fortunes were
linked to the patronage of the crown. In the previous chapter we have
seen that the Chancellor was a proponent of reform—a defender, among
other things, of the judiciary and of the country generally against the
expanding court of the early seventeenth century. However, as paterfamil-
ias and patron of a widespread clientage composed of relatives, friends,
and the friends of relatives, Bellièvre exploited his offices to the full.

Traffic in offices, prebends, and benefices was at the heart of the
patronage system which centered on the court. There were few revenue-
producing offices which were not venal, and the servants of the crown
were among the most favored in the intense competition for the bounty
which the monarchy controlled. Thus, the high judicial offices which
Bellièvre held during the years 1564–70 and 1576–80 had no relationship to his actual functions within the government. There is no evidence
to suggest that he ever resided in Lyons when he occupied the post of
lieutenant general in the *sénéchaussée* of that city.[1] Likewise, he primarily
engaged in the diplomatic and administrative service of the crown at the
time when he was an officer of the Parlement of Paris. In 1580 Bellièvre
sold his office of president of the parlement for the reported sum of
60,000 *livres,* causing Pierre L'Estoile to remark pointedly that the
people of France could indeed expect justice from magistrates who
bought their offices at so dear a price.[2] The diarist's sarcasm was well
taken, for Bellièvre's later offices in the judiciary were largely a form of
patronage tendered by the monarchy to one of its most loyal servants.

Whatever his views on nepotism and venality, Bellièvre skillfully
utilized the existing system of privilege to promote his own fortune, as
well as to place his children in high office and to assure their well-being.
This contrast between the Chancellor's public reputation and his role as
family dynast is best illustrated by an incident which occurred in 1628 and
which pitted Bellièvre's descendants against the *garde des sceaux,* Michel

---

1. On this point, see Maurice Pallasse, *La Sénéchaussée et siège présidial de
Lyon pendant les guerres de religion* (Lyons, 1943), p. 292.
2. L'Estoile, *Journal,* I, 368.

de Marillac. At issue was a councillorship in the Parlement of Paris which Bellièvre's son, Nicolas de Bellièvre, sought for his own son, Pomponne II. To circumvent a rule of parlement against nepotism—Nicolas was a president of the court—a special dispensation was obtained from the crown.[3] Marillac opposed this action and evoked the memory of the Chancellor who, he claimed, would have disapproved of this breakdown of discipline in the sovereign courts.[4] Previously, however, Nicolas de Bellièvre reminded Marillac that it was the Chancellor who had secured an earlier dispensation which had maintained yet another councillorship in the family's hands.[5] Indeed, in 1605, some five years after he had lectured the Parlement of Paris on the evils of nepotism, the Chancellor had intervened with the crown to gain for his youngest son, Nicolas, the right to succeed his brother, Claude II de Bellièvre, as councillor.[6] At the time, Nicolas was less than the age required for entry into the parlement, and his appointment represented the triumph of family interests over the ancient rules of the court.

Another incident, which took place in 1590, provides an insight into the commercial aspects of officeholding as it was practiced by the Bellièvres. In that year, Bellièvre's son-in-law, Claude Prévost de Saint-Cyre, died. From his estate at Grignon, Bellièvre beseeched the King and his friends at the royal court to preserve for his daughter the profits from the sale of Saint-Cyre's office of *maître des requêtes*.[7] The matter was taken up in the *Conseil d'état,* and the request was approved.[8] Bellièvre apparently charged his nephew, Charles Faye, with the responsibility of selling his son-in-law's office. In August 1591, Faye wrote his uncle, "Regarding the office of the late Monsieur de Saint-Cyre, I spoke to a Gascon who has written to Bordeaux and has found me a man who will

3. B.N., Ms. fr. 16484, fol. 355, Louis XIII to the Parlement of Paris, 16 February 1629.

4. *Ibid.,* fol. 363, Marillac to Nicolas de Bellièvre, 24 June 1628.

5. *Ibid.,* fol. 362, Nicolas de Bellièvre to Marillac, 1 June 1628.

6. Edouard Maugis, *Histoire du Parlement de Paris de l'avènement des rois Valois à la mort d'Henri IV* (Paris, 1913–16), II, 214, 226; III, 320.

7. B.N., Ms. fr. 15892, fol. 301, Bellièvre to d'O, 9 December 1590; Ms. fr. 15909, fol. 435, Bellièvre to Henry IV, December 1590.

8. B.N., Ms. fr. 15911, fol. 421, Cheverny to Madame de Bellièvre, December 1590.

pay up to 4,500 *livres.*"[9] Faye also announced that he had gone to Chartres to interview other prospective purchasers. Such concessions regarding offices were among the rewards for loyalty and service to the crown.

The Church also provided the monarchy with a rich source of patronage, and Bellièvre was among the most assiduous in searching out ecclesiastical benefices for his family. In 1573 the royal councillor apparently desired to obtain a benefice belonging to the recently deceased Cardinal of Ferrara, for in January of that year Catherine de Medici informed him that the papacy had disposed of the late cardinal's holdings and that she was unable to satisfy his request.[10] On another occasion, Catherine wrote to the Duke of Epernon, "and I think that, having for a long time promised the King . . . to give to Monsieur Bellièvre some benefices for one of his sons . . . this opportunity would be appropriate and would not inconvenience the King."[11] The details of this transaction are lacking, but Bellièvre's acquisition of the Abbey of Jouay is fully documented. Shortly after his retirement from the court in 1588, Bellièvre entered into a complex series of negotiations with the monarchy and the papacy to secure this richly endowed abbey for his son Albert.[12] In this case a special dispensation was required because of the younger Bellièvre's age. Having obtained letters patent from the crown, Bellièvre then sought papal approval. To the French ambassador in Rome he wrote, "I beg also that my son be dispensed . . . because of his age, for he has not yet reached eighteen years. This is something which is often granted. Monsieur Brulart . . . has obtained a similar grace for his son." Albert de Bellièvre, future Archbishop of Lyons, acquired the Abbey of Jouay which, through the device of reversions, remained in the family's patrimony well into the seventeenth century.

Something of the family's acquisitive temper, as it was directed to the procurement of benefices, is revealed in the correspondence of Jacques Faye with his uncle. At one point in the 1570's (the exact date is not

9. *Lettres inédites de Jacques et de Charles Faye,* ed. E. Halphen (Paris, 1880), p. 119. (Hereafter cited as *Lettres Faye.*)

10. *Lettres de Catherine de Médicis,* ed. H. de la Ferrière (Paris, 1891), IV, 152.

11. *Ibid.,* VII, 415.

12. B.N., Ms. fr. 22897, fols. 19–22, Bellièvre to the Marquis of Pisany, 28 November 1588.

certain) Faye wrote Bellièvre of the death of the Bishop and Count of Noyon, possessor of a bishopric with "very handsome seignioral rights." "Because vacant benefices do not appear every day," he advised his uncle, "you must omit nothing in order to have it." Shortly thereafter, Bellièvre was informed that the Bishop of Noyon was, in fact, alive. Faye apologized for his error, reported that the bishopric was worth eight or nine thousand francs annually, and urged his uncle to watch the situation carefully, "for the man is old, and what did not happen today might happen in a month." [13]

In addition to his responsibility for placing and maintaining his numerous children, Bellièvre served as the principal patron of that group of interrelated families over which he presided by right of eminence. These were primarily magisterial families, located in the south and in Paris, which were dependent upon the favors and privileges granted the Chancellor by the crown. A nephew, Ennemond Rabot, once wrote Bellièvre, "After God our principal recourse is to you." [14] A few examples illustrating Bellièvre's use of his high position to further the interests of those who composed his personal clientage will bear out the essential truth of Rabot's remark.

Shortly after entering the *Conseil d'état* and the administrative service of the Valois monarchy, Bellièvre arranged for the appointment of his brother, Jean Bellièvre-Hautefort, as president of the Parlement of Grenoble and for the succession of his nephew, Artus II Prunier, to Hautefort's office of councillor in the parlement. [15] In the same year, 1571, Bellièvre obtained for his nephew, Ennemond Rabot, a dispensation from the law which forbade the simultaneous occupation of judicial offices by father and son. [16] When Rabot died in 1603, the Chancellor intervened with the King to secure for his wife and son-in-law substantial compensation for the loss of the judicial office. [17] Bellièvre was also instrumental in placing Rabot's office of first president in the hands of Artus II Prunier. [18] On

13. *Lettres Faye*, pp. 9, 16.
14. B.N., Ms. fr. 15911, fol. 363, Rabot to Bellièvre, September 1588.
15. B.N., Ms. fr. 15901, fol. 110, Artus II Prunier to Bellièvre, 21 May 1571.
16. *Ibid.*, fol. 101, Laurent Rabot to Bellièvre, May 1571.
17. B.N., Ms. fr. 15976, fol. 481, Bellièvre to Beaumont, 22 November 1603.
18. B.N., Ms. fr. 15898, fol. 455, Artus II Prunier to Bellièvre, December 1603.

another occasion, Henry IV granted to Guillaume de Faye the right to resign an abbey to a young relative. The royal letters patent specifically mentioned that this was done as a favor for Faye's uncle, the Chancellor.[19] Characteristically, one of Bellièvre's last acts before his death was to assure that this abbey would remain in his family.[20]

Families even more remote from the Chancellor than the Pruniers, Fayes, and Rabots turned to Bellièvre to promote their interests at court. Concerning the wish of the Archbishop of Vienne to resign his post to a brother, Bellièvre wrote the following to Henry IV: [21]

> May it be Your Majesty's good will to favor him, granting the resigna-
> tion which the archbishop, his brother, has made in his favor. . . .
> About which I shall humbly pray to Your Majesty because his uncle
> was a good friend . . . also because one of his brothers, lieutenant
> general in the *sénéchaussée,* has married the daughter of my cousin. . . .

At another time, Bellièvre invoked the marriage tie between a cousin and the son of an officer in the Parlement of Grenoble in order to secure a special privilege for the magistrate.[22] These, and other examples which might be cited, amply demonstrate that the benefits deriving from Bellièvre's influence at court extended well beyond his immediate family to all those who were bound to him by ties of blood and marriage. The privileges accorded this vast family were a measure of the Chancellor's personal prestige and power at the royal court.

The privileges which belonged to those who comprised the court sustained the Bellièvre dynasty. If Henry IV rewarded his councillor and Chancellor with large salaries, the Bellièvre family nonetheless remained dependent upon those extraordinary favors which derived from the court connection.[23] Even lavish gifts from the crown, such as one of 24,000 *livres* granted the Chancellor in 1602,[24] came from the sale of offices in the royal administration. Thus, the fortunes of the Bellièvres were inextri-

19. B.N., Ms. fr. 15896, fol. 85.

20. Jacques Davy Du Perron, *Les Diverses Oeuvres de Cardinal Du Perron* (Paris, 1623), I, 615.

21. B.N., Ms. fr. 15893, fol. 229, Bellièvre to Henry IV, 7 March 1595.

22. *Ibid.,* fol. 270, Bellièvre to Villeroy, 26 June 1595.

23. It appears that Bellièvre received 9,000 *livres* annually for his service in Lyons and 24,000 *livres* annually as chancellor.

24. B.N., PO. 280, nos. 93, 94.

cably bound to the court as it was—a corrupt, venal, and, for the country, expensive institution.

II

ECONOMIC PRIVILEGE, preferment in the highly competitive race for offices, and social prestige were among the advantages which came to Bellièvre and his family through the court connection. Each comprised part of the legacy of power which the Chancellor passed on to his heirs, and it is with a brief sketch of this legacy that we conclude our study of his life.

As was true of other great officeholding families, the economic life of the Bellièvres was based not only upon office and its privileges but also upon land. From the time of his entry into the King's service, Bellièvre diligently expanded his family's property holdings, particularly in the Ile-de-France. His principal agent was Jacques Faye, who toured the country seeking suitable properties.[25] Together with his principal estate of Grignon, the Chancellor owned numerous seigniories and fiefs. In 1604, at the time of his marriage to Claude Brulart, Nicolas de Bellièvre was named heir to the fief, land, and seigniory of Carcassonne; farms and fiefs in the village of Marq; the fief and farm of Monmoulin; and two fiefs and a country house situated "outside the Gate of the Temple in Paris." In addition, Nicolas received two houses on the Rue de Bethisy, the location of the Chancellor's Parisian residence.[26] His inheritance, in land alone, was valued at 120,000 *livres*.[27] Among other properties left by the Chancellor were two buildings in Lyons, the chateau of Milan, and the Golden Eagle.[28]

In addition to the landed property which the Chancellor bequeathed to his children, there were *rentes* constituted on the *Hôtel de Ville* and large cash settlements in the form of gifts and dowries.[29] Among the latter, we

25. *Lettres Faye,* pp. 2–3, 5, 9, 12, 16, 28–29.
26. A.N., Y 146, fols. 158ᵛ–60.
27. B.N., Cab. H. 69, fol. 30.
28. A.N., Y 170, fol. 470.
29. There is little information on the role of *rentes* in Bellièvre's fortune. The few receipts which have survived indicate a heavy investment in 1573 (B.N., PO. 280, nos. 74, 76, 78, 79, 82, 85).

143

find a gift of 50,000 *livres* bestowed upon Nicolas de Bellièvre in 1607 and a dowry of 80,000 *livres* presented to a daughter in 1604.[30] If the fragmentary nature of the sources precludes any attempt to calculate Bellièvre's fortune, it is nevertheless apparent that the Chancellor, like his colleagues, expanded his holdings during the course of his career and increased his family's rich inheritance from previous generations.

In an aristocratic society, social rank was as important a form of power as material wealth, and was, moreover, one source of those privileges by which wealth was increased. For certain of the officeholding dynasties of the early seventeenth century, the upper bureaucracy and sovereign courts served as bridges to the more illustrious military aristocracy. The principal heir of Villeroy, for example, was Charles de Neufville, Baron of Magny, Marquis of Halincourt, knight of the Orders of the King, captain of one hundred armed men, and governor of Lyons, Forez, and Beaujolais. His functions, as well as his titles, were those of the *noblesse d'épée*. Sillery's eldest son, Pierre Brulart, bore the titles of Marquis of Sillery and Viscount of Puysieux, but he served the crown in an administrative capacity. Succeeding generations of the family, however, exercised military functions primarily, and, by the later decades of the century, the Brularts de Sillery were firmly entrenched in the *noblesse d'épée*. The Bellièvres, on the other hand, retained their identity as *robins*. The high offices accorded the Chancellor by the crown assured his heirs a ranking place among France's ruling families and a permanent nobility. Entry into the life of the royal court, however, did not detach the Bellièvres from their roots in the *robe longue*.

As the patriarch of a large family, Bellièvre tended to arrange marriage alliances with other officeholding families and to place his sons in the sovereign courts or the Church. Throughout their later history, the Bellièvres continued to base their power upon judicial and ecclesiastical institutions. There was, however, a conspicuous rise in the prestige and importance of the offices held by the children and grandchildren of the Chancellor. Not the least of the advantages of the court connection was the preferment which the family received in the matter of placement. Whereas earlier Bellièvres had occupied minor ecclesiastical positions in

30. A.N., Y 142, fol. 377; Y 146, fol. 160.

Lyons, two of the Chancellor's sons were archbishops of the city. Albert de Bellièvre was appointed archbishop in 1599, and, according to one account, having become imbecile, he resigned his office to his brother, Claude de Bellièvre, councillor in the Parlement of Paris.[31] The latter remained archbishop from 1605 until his death in 1612. Preferment and nepotism also played a large part in the career of Nicolas de Bellièvre, youngest of the Chancellor's three sons, who continued the family's tradition of officeholding in the sovereign courts. Nicolas, as we have seen, entered the Parlement of Paris in 1605, replacing Claude II de Bellièvre as councillor. In 1614 he received the rights to the office of president of the parlement, which he occupied until 1642, when the office passed to his son, Pomponne II de Bellièvre.[32] During the half century after the Chancellor's death, his descendants established themselves as one of the most powerful of the dynasties in the Parlement of Paris. The tradition of the *robe longue* was another important legacy bequeathed to his posterity by the Chancellor.

III

POMPONNE DE BELLIÈVRE, servant of five kings and family dynast, died in Paris early in September 1607. He was buried in the chapel of the church of Saint-Germain L'Auxerrois, close to the palace of the monarchs whom he had served. Power had long since passed from the Chancellor's hands, and the government was dominated by his rival, Sully, during the last years of Henry's reign. Yet Sillery, Villeroy, and Jeannin remained among the leading advisers of the King and maintained their powers after Sully's fall from grace. These three, together with the Chancellor, were the most eminent heirs of that tradition of crown service represented in an earlier age by L'Hôpital, Morvillier, Bochetel, and the L'Aubespines. In an era when the modern concept of a civil service was neither thought of nor possible, the high officers provided that essential continuity in administration and expertise in political affairs necessary to the maintenance of government. The members of this elite were not men of humble origins, nor were they the shock troops of monarchical despotism. Rather, they

31. B.N., Ms. fr., nouv. acq. 9655, fol. 82.
32. B.N., PO. 280, no. 117.

145

were men born to privilege and trained to serve under the crown. Each had a keen sense of his own self-interest; each was influenced, at least in part, by loyalties to class, to family, and even to patrons other than the king. They were the king's men, but they were also part of a privileged order with its own interests and style of life to defend. It was this mixing of public power and private interest which gave the administrative system of the early modern period its distinctive coloration.

Within the officeholding class, the *robe longue* stood as the dominant element. From its ranks were drawn many of the monarchy's councillors, diplomats, and agents. By the late sixteenth century, the robe had achieved a sense of corporate pride, identity, and interest which found expression in the words and deeds of its most notable representative at court, the Chancellor. He was, as Roland Mousnier has noted, the conscience of the robe.[33] His devotion to the law and the customary constitution of the realm, along with more practical considerations, placed him among the loyalists during the religious wars. The same values, in turn, made him an exponent of monarchy limited by the law. If his conception of the social order was static and his longing for the restoration of the old ways quixotic, Bellièvre nonetheless clearly perceived that tension between public power and the law which marked the constitutional and political history of the absolutist era.

From 1570, when Bellièvre entered the councils of the crown, until the capitulation of Mayenne in 1596, the old order and the old laws which commanded his loyalties were severely challenged by civil rebellion. Whatever the ties of patronage and self-interest which bound him to the court, Bellièvre was a *politique* out of conviction. The coming of domestic peace, however, raised a new and less dramatic set of constitutional questions concerning the relationship of the King to the law and the structure of royal government. As Chancellor, Bellièvre utilized his high office to assure that the rule of law would encompass crown and country alike. This was to be accomplished through the crown's self-restraint, through the device of conciliar government, and through the reformation of the legal order. At the height of his quarrel with Sully, the Chancellor had written Villeroy, "The blame which the Parlement re-

33. "Sully et Le Conseil d'état et des finances: la lutte entre Bellièvre et Sully," *Revue historique,* CXLII (1941), 85.

ceives derives from the incapacity and the malice of the officers who are placed there. If the King does not heed the prayers of his chancellor, then his chancellor will be discharged before God and before His Majesty of responsibility for the faults of his officers." [34] He was not, then, the spokesman for all of the officers, but for those men of "quality" whose traditional function it was to judge in the king's courts and to administer the king's affairs. By the monarchy, he was honored and rewarded for his good service in the councils, in the field, and abroad. By the *robe longue*, he was rightly remembered as the protector of the magistrates and of the king's justice.

34. B.N., Ms. fr. 15894, fol. 564, Bellièvre to Villeroy, 30 May 1603.

BIBLIOGRAPHY

I. Unpublished Primary Sources

THE PRINCIPAL SOURCE on the Chancellor's life is the collection of papers at the *Bibliothèque Nationale,* which comprises *Manuscrits français* 15890 to 15912 and 16013–16023. Volumes 15890–15894 contain Bellièvre's letters and public papers for the years 1566–1606. Many of these documents are originals. Volume 15895 consists of seventeenth-century copies of his major addresses and public letters. Letters addressed to Bellièvre during his chancellorship are to be found in *Manuscrits français* 15896–15900. The following eleven volumes include letters sent to Bellièvre between 1562 and 1599. Copies of papers relating to his intendancy in Lyons are collected in volume 15912. *Manuscrits français* 16013–16023 are a valuable source on Bellièvre's service as ambassador in Switzerland. Other series at the *Bibliothèque Nationale* supplement the main body of Bellièvre manuscripts. Among the more important of these are the following: on Bellièvre's intendancy in Lyons, *Fonds Dupuy* 64; on the negotiations with Casimir and Condé in 1576, *Fonds Dupuy* 502 and *Cinq Cents de Colbert* 8. Documents on the economic and social aspects of the Chancellor's life are included in Volume 280 of the *Pièces originales* at the *Bibliothèque Nationale.*

II. Printed Source Materials

BELLIÈVRE, POMPONNE DE. "Contre la Paulette: mémoire du Chancelier Bellièvre," ed. ET. FAGES, *Revue Henri IV,* I (1906), 182–88.
———. "Lettre confidentielle de Bellièvre sur le cahier de l'Assemblée du Clergé de 1595," ed. ALBERT CHAMBERLAND, *Revue Henry IV,* III (1912), 257–74.
———. "Lettre inédite de M. de Bellièvre au Roi Henri IV au sujet de l'emprisonnement du Duc de Nemours," *Revue du Lyonnais,* XVI (1858), 81–83.

————. "Lettres inédites de M. de Bellièvre au Roi Henri IV au sujet de l'emprisonnement du Duc de Nemours," *Revue du Lyonnais*, XVII (1858), 306–16.

————, and NICOLAS BRULART DE SILLERY, *Mémoires de Bellièvre et de Silleri*. 2 vols. Amsterdam, 1696.

BERNARD, AUGUSTE, ed. *Procès-verbaux des états généraux de 1593*. Paris, 1842.

*Catalogue des actes de François Ier*. 10 vols. Paris, 1887–1908.

FAYE, JACQUES, and CHARLES FAYE. *Lettres inédites de Jacques et de Charles Faye*, ed. E. HALPHEN. Paris, 1880.

GACHARD, M., ed. *Actes des états généraux des pays-bas, 1576–1585*. Vol. I. Brussels, 1861.

GUÉRIN, PAUL, *et al.*, eds. *Registres des délibérations du Bureau de la Ville de Paris*. 19 vols. Paris, 1883–1958.

HENRY III. *Lettres de Henri III, Roi de France*, ed. PIERRE CHAMPION. Vol. I. Paris, 1959.

HENRY IV. *Lettres inédites du Roi Henri IV au Chancelier de Bellièvre*, ed. E. HALPHEN. 5 vols. Paris, 1872–1883.

————. *Recueil des lettres missives de Henri IV*, eds. BERGER DE XIVREY and J. GAUDET. 9 vols. Paris, 1843–1876.

LOMAS, SOPHIE CRAWFORD, and RICHARD B. WERNHAM, eds. *Calendar of State Papers, Foreign Series, the Reign of Elizabeth*. Vols. XVIII (1914), XIX (1916), XXI (1927), XXII (1936). London, 1907—.

MÉDICIS, CATHERINE DE. *Lettres de Catherine de Médicis*, eds. H. DE LA FERRIÈRE and COUNT BAGUENAULT DE PUCHESSE. 10 vols. Paris, 1880–1909.

TEULET, ALEXANDRE, ed. *Relations politiques de la France et de l'Espagne avec l'Ecosse au XVIe siècle*. Vol. IV. Paris, 1862.

VALOIS, NOËL, ed. *Inventaire des arrêts du Conseil d'Etat, règne de Henri IV*. 2 vols. Paris, 1886–1893.

III. *Memoirs and Diaries*

1. Principal collections

MICHAUD and POUJOULAT, eds. *Nouvelle Collection des mémoires relatifs à l'histoire de France*. 34 vols. Paris, 1881.

JEANNIN, PIERRE. *Négociations du Président Jeannin*. Vol. XVIII.

SULLY, *Mémoires des sages et royales oeconomies d'estat de Henri le Grand*. Vols. XVI–XVII.

PETITOT, M., ed. *Collection Complète des mémoires relatifs à l'histoire de France*. 52 vols. Paris, 1820–1829.

FONTENAY-MAREUIL. *Mémoires de Messire du Val, Marquis de Fontenay-Mareuil.* Vols. L–LI.

HURAULT, PHILIPPE. *Mémoires de Messire Philippe Hurault, Comte de Cheverny.* Vol. XXXV.

PALMA CAYET. *Chronologie novenaire.* Vol. XLI.

VILLEROY, NICOLAS. *Mémoires d'estat.* Vol. XXXVI.

2. Other Memoirs

BASSOMPIERRE. *Mémoires du Maréchal de Bassompierre,* ed. M. DE CHANTÉRAC. 2 vols. Paris, 1870.

BELLIÈVRE, CLAUDE. *Souvenirs de voyages en Italie et en Orient, notes historiques, pièces de vers,* ed. CHARLES PERRAT. Geneva, 1956.

GASSOT, JULES. *Sommaire mémorial de Jules Gassot, secrétaire du roi,* ed. PIERRE CHAMPION. Paris, 1934.

L'ESTOILE, PIERRE. *Journal de L'Estoile pour le règne de Henri IV,* ed. LOUIS-RAYMOND LEFÈVRE. 2 vols. Paris, 1948—.

IV. *Secondary Works*

THE FOLLOWING LIST is a highly selective one and includes only those books and articles which bear directly upon Bellièvre's career or upon the institutions in which he served.

BLOCH, JEAN-RICHARD, *L'Anoblissement en France au temps de François Ier.* Paris, 1934.

CHAMBERLAND, ALBERT. "Le Conseil des finances en 1596 et 1597 et *les economies royales,*" *Revue Henri IV,* I (1905–1906), 20–32, 152–63, 250–60, 274–84.

CHARLÉTY, SÉBASTIEN. *Histoire de Lyon depuis les origines jusqu'à nos jours.* Lyons, 1903.

CHURCH, WILLIAM F. *Constitutional Thought in Sixteenth Century France: A Study in the Evolution of Ideas.* Cambridge, 1941.

COURBIS, EUGÈNE. *La Municipalité lyonnaise sous l'ancien régime.* Lyons, 1900.

DÉNIAU, JEAN. *La Commune de Lyon et la guerre bourguignonne.* Lyons, 1934.

DOUCET, ROGER. *Finances municipales et crédit public à Lyon au XVIe siècle.* Paris, 1937.

———. *Les Institutions de la France au XVIe siècle.* 2 vols. Paris, 1948.

DROUOT, HENRI. *Mayenne et la bourgogne: étude sur la ligue.* 2 vols. Paris, 1937.

FÉDOU, RENÉ. *Les Hommes de loi lyonnais à la fin du moyen age: étude sur les origines de la classe de robe.* Paris, 1964.

GARNIER, NOËL. *"Le Président Jeannin,"* *Mémoires de la Société Bourguignonne de Géographie et d'Histoire,* XXVIII (1913), 287–589.

GIESEY, RALPH. "The Juristic Basis of Dynastic Right to the French Throne," *Transactions of the American Philosophical Society,* LI, Pt. 5 (1961), 25–38.

HANOTAUX, GABRIEL. *Origines de l'institution des intendants des provinces.* Paris, 1884.

IMBART DE LA TOUR, P. *Les Origines de la réforme.* 2d ed. 4 vols. Melun, 1948.

JENSEN, DE LAMAR. *Diplomacy and Dogmatism: Bernardino de Mendoza and the French Catholic League.* Cambridge, 1964.

KLEINCLAUSZ, A. *Histoire de Lyon.* 3 vols. Lyons, 1939–1952.

MARIÉJOL, JEAN. *Catherine de Médicis.* Paris, 1920.

———. "La Réforme et la ligue—l'édit de Nantes, 1559–1598," *Histoire de France depuis les origines jusqu'à la révolution,* ed. ERNEST LAVISSE. Vol. VI. Paris, 1911.

MATTINGLY, GARRETT. *The Armada.* Boston, 1959.

MAUGIS, EDOUARD. *Histoire du parlement de Paris de l'avènement des rois Valois à la mort d'Henri IV.* 3 vols. Paris, 1913–1916.

MONNIER, LOUIS. "Les Missions diplomatiques de Pomponne de Bellièvre de 1573 à 1588," *Ecole Nationale des Chartes, positions des thèses.* Paris, 1930, 119–28.

MOUSNIER, ROLAND. *La Vénalité des offices sous Henri IV et Louis XIII.* Rouen, 1946.

———. "Le Conseil du roi de la mort de Henri IV au gouvernement personnel de Louis XIV," *Etudes d'histoire moderne et contemporaine,* I (1947), 29–67.

———. "Sully et le Conseil d'Etat et des finances: la lutte entre Bellièvre et Sully," *Revue historique,* CXLII (1941), 68–86.

NEALE, J. E. *The Age of Catherine de Medici.* New York, 1958.

NOUAILLAC, J. "La Retraite de Pomponne de Bellièvre," *Revue historique,* CXVII (1914), 129–67.

———. *Villeroy, secrétaire d'état et ministre de Charles IX, Henri III et Henri IV.* Paris, 1909.

PALLASSE, MAURICE. *La Sénéchaussée et siège présidial de Lyon pendant les guerres de religion.* Lyons, 1943.

PERRAT, CHARLES. "Claude Bellièvre et Etienne Dolet," *Bibliothèque d'humanisme et renaissance,* IV (1944), 138–43.

———. "Les Humanistes amateurs de papyrus," *Bibliothèque de l'école des Chartes,* CIX (1951), 173–92.

POIRSON, AUGUSTE. *Histoire du règne de Henri IV.* 2d ed. 4 vols. Paris, 1862.

RICHARD, P. *Pierre d'Epinac, archevêque de Lyon, 1573–1599.* Paris, n.d.

ROMIER, LUCIEN. *Le Royaume de Catherine de Médicis.* 2 vols. Paris, 1922.

ROTT, EDOUARD. *Histoire de la représentation diplomatique de la France auprès les cantons suisses.* 10 vols. Paris, 1902–1935.

SCHNAPPER, BERNARD. *Les Rentes au XVIᵉ siècle: histoire d'un instrument de crédit.* Paris, 1957.

SUTHERLAND, N. M. *The French Secretaries of State in the Age of Catherine de Medici.* London, 1962.

VALOIS, NOËL. *Le Conseil du Roi.* Paris, 1888.

VAN DYKE, PAUL. *Catherine de Médicis.* 2 vols. New York, 1927.

ZELLER, GASTON. *Les Institutions de la France au XVIᵉ siècle.* Paris, 1948.

INDEX

Albert, Cardinal-Archduke of Austria, 100, 102

Anjou, Francis of Valois, Duke of: Bellièvre's negotiations with in 1581, 43; his death, 45; leader of the "malcontents," 38, 39; and the Low Countries, 40, 42; and the Norman League, 40–41; and the Peace of Fleix, 41

Aumale, Duke of, 51

Bassompierre, Marshal, 135

Belin, Count of, 72, 73

Bellièvre, Albert de, 140, 145

Bellièvre, Barthélemy I, 9–10, 11

Bellièvre, Barthélemy II, 11, 16*n*

Bellièvre, Claude, 11, 12, 16, 16*n;* crown service, 15–16; and the humanists of Lyons, 13

Bellièvre, Claude II de, 145

Bellièvre, family of: and the *Consulat* of Lyons, 10–11; education and cultural life, 13; marriage alliances, 12–13; offices and social status, 20; origins, 9; and patrimonial officeholding, 11–12; and the patronage of the Church, 11–12; properties, 12, 12*n*

Bellièvre, Hugonin, 9, 10, 11

Bellièvre, Jean de, 17, 17*n*, 22, 141

Bellièvre, Nicolas de, 134, 139, 143, 145

Bellièvre, Pomponne de: his character, 33–34; death of, 145; early years, 24–25; enters parlement, 17; family patron, 141–42; judicial offices, 25*n;* landholdings, 143; member of *Conseil d'affaires,* 6; relations with Jean Morvillier, 26–27; retires to Grignon, 56–58; and royal patronage, 21, 138–42; Stafford's opinion of, 29; wealth a factor in his rise, 25–26

—and the later Valois: administrator of finances, 37, 37*n;* ambassador to Poland, 37–38; ambassador to Switzerland, 30–31, 32; dismissed by Henry III, 52–53, 54; on judicial reform, 36; mission to Elizabeth I, 49–50; mission to the Low Countries in 1578, 40; negotiates the Peace of Fleix, 41; negotiations with the Duke of Anjou, 40–41, 43; negotiations with Duke Jean Casimir, 38–40; negotiations with the Dukes of Guise and Mayenne, 50–52; negotiations with Henry of Navarre and the Huguenots, 44–45; promoted to royal council, 32; reconciles Henry of Navarre and Marguerite of Valois, 44–45; seeks conversion of Henry of Navarre, 46–47; seeks to enforce Peace of Felix, 42–43; seeks reconciliation of Henry III and Henry of Navarre, 48; on the unification of Christendom, 34–35

—and Henry IV: at conference of Suresnes, 70–72; conflict with Ornano, 79; connections in the Catholic League, 68; and the *Conseil des finances,* 94, 96–98; on the conversion of Henry IV, 66; directs Henry IV's attention to south, 83–84; discourse against the Estates of the League, 63–65; and dissolution of Henry IV's marriage, 100; and the Edict of Nantes, 98–99; and Henry of Montmorency, 82–83; intendant of Lyons, 76–89; mission to Mayenne, 72, 74;

155

negotiations with Epernon, 81–82; negotiations with Nemours, 80–81; on obedience to papacy, 64–65, 66–67; police functions in Lyons, 86–87; his pragmatism, 93–94; public letter to Jeannin, 61–62; range of duties as councillor, 92–93; and reconstruction in Lyons, 85–86; reforms civil government of Lyons, 88–89; on religious divisions in France, 94; reports on military affairs, 84–85; seeks to extend truce of 1593, 73; seeks favor of court, 69; supports Henry IV's claim to throne, 59; and treaty of Vervins, 100–102
—Chancellor of Henry IV: on administrative reform, 128–29; appointed chancellor, 104; conflicts with Sully, 125–34; criticized by Henry IV, 126–27; defender of *robe longue,* 132–33; duties of office, 105–6, 116; and judicial administration, 117–19; and judicial officers, 118; loss of power, 133–36; opposes war with Savoy, 125; opposition to acts of Henry IV, 108–9, 110, 111–13; and the parlements, 113–15, 119; against the *Paulette,* 130–34; presides over council, 120–21; on reform of judicial system, 107; response to appointment, 106–7; seeks to restore powers of council, 129–30; and trial of Biron, 117; views on foreign policy, 127–28
Bellièvre, Pomponne II de, 139
Biron, Marshal, 85, 102, 117
Bochetel, Guillaume, 18
Bouillon, Duke of, 50
Bourges, Archbishop of, 70, 71
Brulart de Sillery, family of, 15*n;* changing social status, 144; landholdings, 22; officeholding, 19
Brulart de Sillery, Nicolas, 91, 122, 123; becomes chancellor, 136; member of *Conseil d'affaires,* 6, 92; named *garde des sceaux,* 134; negotiates Treaty of Vervins, 100–102; offices in parlement, 19; and royal patronage, 21

Calatagirone, Bonaventura, negotiations with Bellièvre, 100
Casimir, Duke Jean, Bellièvre's negotiations with, 38–40
Chancellorship, the nature of the office, 104–6

Cheverny, Philippe Hurault, Count of, 52–53, 90, 103, 106
Clement VIII, 64, 67, 70, 71
Clervant, Jean de, 46
Conseil d'affaires, 4, 5–6, 122–23
Conseil d'état et des finances, 4, 5
Conseil des finances, under Henry IV, 94–98
Consulat of Lyons, 10–11; reformed by Bellièvre, 88–89

Duplessis-Mornay, Philippe de, 60

Elizabeth I, Bellièvre's mission to, 49
Epernon, Duke of, Bellièvre's negotiations with, 81–82
Epinac, Pierre d', 58; at conference of Suresnes, 70–71; and government of Lyons, 77; on religion in the state, 68–69

Faye, Charles, 139–40
Faye, Jacques, 53, 140, 141
Fleix, Peace of, 41
Forget de Fresnes, Pierre, 82

Gondi, Cardinal de, 68, 70
Guise, Henry, Duke of: and the Day of the Barricades, 51–52; negotiations with Catherine de Medici and Bellièvre, 50, 51; and Philip II, 47; and the Treaty of Nemours, 46–47

Henry III, King of France and Poland, 37, 38, 45; dismisses councillors and secretaries, 52–53; and Henry of Navarre, 48; sends Bellièvre to Mayenne, 50
Henry IV, King of France and Navarre, 3, 5, 6, 76, 77, 78, 81, 83, 86, 88, 91, 92, 98, 99, 104, 113, 116; and the administration of justice, 108–10, 111, 112, 119; and Bellièvre, 93, 96, 126; and Bellièvre's decline, 134–35; Bellièvre's negotiations with, 43–45; Bellièvre's opinion of, 42; on Bellièvre's qualifications as chancellor, 106; concept of kingship, 121–22; conflicts with parlements, 114–15; and *Conseil d'affaires,* 122–23; and *Conseil des finances,* 95, 97–98; conversion in 1593, 66, 71; defines powers of intendant, 79–80; delays negotiations with

Spain, 101; dissolution of marriage, 100; objectives of his diplomacy at Vervins, 101; protects Huguenots of Dauphiné, 44, 45; sends Bellièvre to Mayenne, 74; sends Biron south, 85; and Treaty of Vervins, 101, 102

Intendancy, evolution of in sixteenth century, 76–77

Jeannin, Pierre, 6, 15, 73, 122, 123; defends Mayenne, 60–61; enters service of Henry IV, 91–92; office and status, 20; and royal patronage, 21
Joinville, Treaty of, 47

La Guiche, Philbert de, 51
Lange, Nicolas de, 78
L'Aubespine, Claude II de, 18, 22
L'Aubespine, family of, 14, 18, 20
L'Aubespine, Guillaume, French ambassador to England, 49
L'Aubespine, Sébastien, 26
L'Hôpital, Michel, 25, 105, 106
Louise of Vaudémont, queen of Henry III, 99
Lyons: conditions in 1594, 78–79; economic conditions, 86; military situation in 1594, 84; municipal government, 10; a plan for its reconstruction, 78; reformation of civil government, 88–89; submits to Henry IV, 76, 77

Marguerite of Valois, Queen of Navarre, 42, 44–45, 46, 100
Marillac, Michel, 139
Mayenne, Charles of Lorraine, Duke of, 70, 73, 74, 77, 91, 99; accepts truce, 73; Bellièvre's negotiations with, 50–51; summons Estates General, 63
Medici, Alexander de, 100, 101
Medici, Catherine de, 48; her agents, 33; Bellièvre's patroness, 31–32; negotiations with Guise, 46–47, 50, 52; orders Bellièvre to Guienne, 41; and patronage, 140; her politics assessed, 54
Mendoza, Bernardino de, and Bellièvre's mission to Elizabeth, 49
Monsieur, Peace of, 39
Montfort, royalist meeting at, 70
Montmorency, Henry of, 6, 84; collaborates with Bellièvre, 82

Morvillier, Jean, Bellièvre's patron, 26–27

Nantes, Edict of, 98
Nemours, Duke of, 87; governor of Lyons, 77; negotiations with Bellièvre, 80–81
Nemours, Treaty of, 46–47
Neufville, Charles de, 144
Neufville, family of, 14, 17–18, 20, 22
Neufville-Villeroy, Nicolas III de, 6, 63, 68, 70, 73, 122, 123, 126, 127, 130; and the Catholic League, 57, 58, 59, 90–91; dismissed by Henry III, 52–53; enters service of Henry IV, 91; negotiates the Peace of Fleix, 41; negotiator for the League, 60; office-holding, 18; Stafford's opinion of, 29
Nevers, Duke of, 70, 74

O, François d', 94
Ornano, Alphonse, 81, 88; conflict with Bellièvre, 79; governor of Lyons, 77

Paulette, debate on, 130–34
Philip II, King of Spain, 100; Bellièvre's accusations against, 66; relations with the Catholic League, 47
Pinart, Claude, 52–53
Prunier, Artus, 141

Rabot, Ennemond, 141
Revol, Louis, 73
Richardot, Jean, 101

Saint-Cyre, Claude de, 139
Schomberg, Gaspard, 39
Sillery. *See* Brulart de Sillery
Stafford, Sir Edward, 29, 33, 49
Sully, Maximilien de Béthune, Duke of, 6, 111, 113, 121, 122, 123, 128, 129, 132, 133, 134; and Bellièvre, 124; conflict with Bellièvre, 125–34; and *Conseil des finances*, 95, 97; and the *Paulette*, 130–34; his scorn for King's councillors, 4, 125; views on foreign policy, 127–28
Suresnes, conference of, 70–72; declaration of royal officials at, 71–72

Taxis, Jean-Baptiste de, 101

Verneuil, Marquise of, 113
Vervins, Treaty of, 100–102
Villeroy. *See* Neufville-Villeroy